The Tiger
Symbol of Freedom

Also by Nicholas Courtney

The Self-Catering Holiday Guide to Shopping and Cooking in Europe

The Tiger
Symbol of Freedom

Nicholas Courtney

Quartet Books
London   Melbourne   New York

First published by Quartet Books Limited 1980
A member of the Namara Group
27 Goodge Street, London W1P 1FD

Copyright © 1980 Nicholas Courtney

ISBN 0 7043 2245 5

Typeset by Trendsetter Photoset Ltd.,
Brentwood, Essex.
Printed in Great Britain by Shenval '80',
Harlow, Essex.

FOR VANESSA

Contents

Illustrations   ix
Acknowledgements   xv
Foreword   1
1   'Tygre: A fierce beast of the leonine kind'   5
2   'There are no tigers in Africa'   9
3   'Tiggers don't climb trees'   17
4   'A chaos of claws, fangs, torsos and backs'   25
5   'Under a pipal tree'   35
6   'There is a raging tiger inside every man'   43
7   'Tiger with lithe and awesome grace'   55
8   'The mark of Wang, King of the Beasts'   61
9   'Shikar!'   71
10   'If all the beasts were gone, man would die'   85
References   101
Bibliography   105

Illustrations

Cover   'The Tiger's Lair' by William Huggins, 1861 *(reproduced by kind permission of Namara Ltd.)*

Black and white

Plate 1   Tiger musing on a rock *(Kailash Sankhala)*
       2   The prowl *(F. W. Champion)*
       3   The tiger drags his kill into the undergrowth *(F. W. Champion)*
       4   The sensitivity of the tiger's whiskers *(F. W. Champion)*
       5   Hunger satisfied for one day *(F. W. Champion)*
       6   Tiger cleaning his claws on the bark of a tree in Chitawan National Park *(Bruce Coleman Ltd, photo: Mary Grant)*
       7   Skull of a hoplophoneus *(reproduced by courtesy of the Trustees of the British Museum, Natural History)*
       8   Head of a cave lion from Dolní Vestoniče *(reproduced by courtesy of the Trustees of the British Museum, Natural History)*
       9   Skull of *Panthera tigris tigris (reproduced by courtesy of the Trustees of the British Museum, Natural History)*
      10   'Walking Tiger', bronze by A. L. Barye *(reproduced by courtesy of the directors of the Sladmore Gallery)*
      11   Tigress statue, 300-200 BC *(The Ny Carlsberg Glyptokek, Copenhagen)*
      12   'Skeleton of a Tiger', anatomical drawing by George Stubbs, 1803 *(reproduced by courtesy of the Trustees of the British Museum)*

13   'Skinned Tiger', anatomical drawing by George Stubbs
          (*reproduced by courtesy of the Trustees of the British Museum*)
14   Skeleton of a *Dinictis* foot (*reproduced by courtesy of the
          Trustees of the British Museum, Natural History*)
15   Indian *waghnak*, seventeenth century (*Victoria and
          Albert Museum, Crown Copyright*)
16(a)   Pug marks of a tiger stalking (*F. W. Champion*)
16(b)   Pug marks of a tiger ambling (*F. W. Champion*)
17   Scroll painting of a Muslim riding a spotted tiger god
          from Santal Parganas, Bengal, India, circa 1930
          (*Victoria and Albert Museum, Crown Copyright*)
18   Bronze belt-hook in the form of a leaping tiger from the
          Ordos region (*Raphael Bequest, reproduced by courtesy of
          the Trustees of the British Museum*)
19   Bronze chape from Uzbekistan, central Asia, 1,000-800
          BC (*presented through the National Art Collection Fund by
          Harry Oppenheimer, reproduced by courtesy of the Trustees of
          the British Museum*)
20   Green jade tiger amulet, Chinese, Han dynasty, circa
          AD 100-200 (*Seligman Bequest, reproduced by courtesy of
          Trustees of the British Museum*)
21   Marble tiger, Shang dynasty, 1,300-1,100 BC (*Mrs M.
          Hambleton Bequest, reproduced by courtesy of the Trustees of
          the British Museum*)
22   'A Tiger by a Stream with Bamboo and Waterfall' by
          Mu Ch'i, thirteenth century (*reproduced by courtesy of the
          Trustees of the British Museum*)
23   'A Tigress and Three Cubs' after Chao Yuan, fourteenth
          century (*reproduced by courtesy of the Trustees of the
          British Museum*)
24   Illustration from 'The Tiger and the Fox' by Aesop (*from
          the collection of the author*)

Colour
Plate 25   'Tom Raw in Danger, Tiger Hunting with Elephants'
          (*from the collection of the author*)
26   Gold and enamel pocket watch for the Chinese market,
          early nineteenth century (*reproduced by courtesy of Sotheby,
          Parke Bernet and Co.*)
27   Tipu's Tiger, the man-tiger organ, Mysore, India, circa
          1790 (*Victoria and Albert Museum, Crown Copyright*)
28   Painted enamel on copper snuffbox, south Staffordshire,
          circa 1770 (*Victoria and Albert Museum, Crown Copyright*)

29 The Eighteenth (Royal Irish) Regiment of Foot at the at the storming of the fortress of Amoy, 26 August 1841 *(reproduced by courtesy of the National Army Museum)*

30 Tiger shot from a *machán* *(Mansell Collection)*

31 Charging tiger, Royal Chitawan National Park *(Bruce Coleman Ltd, photo: Mary Grant)*

32 The mark of *wang*, tiger in the Royal Chitawan National Park *(Bruce Coleman Ltd, photo: Mike Price)*

33 Tigress resting, Kanha National Park *(Bruce Coleman Ltd, photo: Peter Jackson)*

34 Tiger fishing? *(Bruce Coleman Ltd, photo: G. D. Plage)*

35 A white tiger of Rewa *(Bruce Coleman Ltd, photo: Peter Jackson)*

36 Tiger courtship *(Kailash Sankhala)*

37 Tigress moving her cubs *(Kailash Sankhala)*

38 The tiger's gait *(Survival Anglia Television, Mike Price)*

Black and white

Plate 39 Tiger-netting in Bengal from the *Illustrated London News*, June 1891 *(Mansell Collection)*

40 Tipu Sultan's throne *(Victoria and Albert Museum, Crown Copyright)*

41 Tipu Sultan's sword *(reproduced by courtesy of Robin Wigington)*

42 Tipu Sultan's banner *(reproduced by gracious permission of of Her Majesty the Queen)*

43 Mortar cast in the form of a seated tiger, Madras 1838 *(reproduced with permission of the controller of Her Majesty's Stationery Office)*

44 Carved tiger stock from Tipu Sultan's sporting gun *(reproduced by courtesy of Robin Wigington)*

45 Lock of Tipu Sultan's sporting gun, showing the tiger cock and tiny tiger safety-catch *(reproduced by courtesy of Robin Wigington)*

46 Earthenware figure of a tiger carrying off a black boy *(reproduced by courtesy of City Museum, Stoke-on-Trent)*

47 Gold tiger's head from Tipu Sultan's throne *(reproduced by gracious permission of Her Majesty the Queen)*

48 'Tigress Attacking a Bullock', mosaic panel from Palazzo dei Conservatori, Rome *(Instituto Archeologic Germanico)*

49 Production still from *Three Weeks*, based on the novel of the same name by Elinor Glyn, 1924 *(British Film Institute)*

50 'The Tiger', lithograph by Edvard Munch, 1909 (*Munch-Museet, Oslo*)

51 'Tiger Devouring a Stag', sculpture by A. L. Barye, 1834 (*Musée des Beaux-Arts, Lyon*)

52 One of a pair of Cloisonné tigers, Chi'ien Lung dynasty, eighteenth century (*Spink and Son, London*)

53 'The Tiger Hunt', Eugène Delacroix in the Louvre, Paris (*Documentation Photographic de la Reunion des Musées Nationaux*)

54 'Tropical Storm with a Tiger' by Henri Rousseau (*National Gallery London, photo: Eileen Tweedy*)

55 Tiger from *Icones Animalium*, 1560 (*Victoria and Albert Museum, Crown Copyright, photo: John Warren*)

56 'The Death of the Royal Tyger', John Zoffany, circa 1795 (*India Office Library and Records*)

57 'The God Shiva, Riding a Tiger, Fighting a Demon', Deccan, India (*reproduced by courtesy of the Trustees of the British Museum*)

58 'The Triumph of Bacchus', mosaic at El Djem, Tunisia (*Musée National du Bardo, Tunis*)

59 Elephant attacking a tiger, engraving (*from the collection of the author, photo: John Warren*)

60 Double-headed Hindu heron being attacked by the Muslim tiger (*reproduced by courtesy of Robin Wigington*)

61 Brooch-pendant of a painted tiger's head in gold setting flanked by four tigers' claws (*Professor and Mrs John Hull Grundy Bequest, reproduced by courtesy of the Trustees of the British Museum*)

62 'Tiger Shooting in India', sketch made during Prince Albert Victor's trip to India, 1890 (*Mansell Collection*)

63 'The Prince's First Tiger', Bounore and Shepherd (*India Office Library and Records*)

64 'Lieutenant Rice and the Tiger', illustration from *Wild Sports of the World* by James Greenwood (*London Library*)

65 Arjan Singh and the tiger cub Tara, Tiger Haven (*Bruce Coleman Ltd, photo: Mike Price*)

Figures

Figure 1 Cave lion engraved on stone slab, La Marche, France
2 Map illustrating the dispersal of the tiger
3 Map showing the approximate world range of the tiger
4 Arms of Lord Milverton (*Debrett's*)

Figure 5   Arms of the de Bardis family
6   Arms of Lord Harris *(Debrett's)*
7   Tigger looking at himself in a broken looking-glass by
     E. H. Shepherd *(Curtis Brown)*
8   *Tigerlillia terribilis* by Edward Lear *(Faber and Faber)*
9   Reserves throughout the tiger's world range

Acknowledgements

The intensive research for my book was made even more enjoyable by the advice and help given by the dozens of experts whom I met or with whom I corresponded. Of these many 'tigerophiles' I would like to thank in particular Dr Charles McDougal for writing the foreword and for reading through the manuscript; Mrs F. W. Champion for permission to use her husband's exquisite photographs; Mr Robin Wigington for his advice and permission to photograph parts of his collection of Tipu Sultan's weaponry. From the Victoria and Albert Museum, London, I would like to thank the assistants in the Indian section and the keeper, Mr Robert Skelton, for permission to photograph 'Tipu's Tiger'; the patient library staff; Miss Anne Buddle from Prints and Drawings and Charles Truman, assistant keeper of the ceramics department. My thanks also go to Dr Andrew Curan and Dr Rosemary Powers of the Natural History Museum who kindly steered me through the tiger's evolution and Miss Tina Millar from Sotheby's and Anthony Spink from Spink and Son who came up with some unusual photographs. Carol O'Calaghan, librarian to Survival Anglia Television, produced the footage for the film strip of the tiger's gait. The illustrations in this book are greatly enhanced by Kailash Sankhala's excellent photographs.

I am much indebted to Sir Geoffry Keynes, chairman of the William Blake Trust for his consent to reproduce 'The Tiger'.

Finally, I would like to thank Lord Harris and the Reverend the Lord Milverton for their consent to reproduce their coats of arms and Debrett's for their permission to use their illustrations.

Few animals have captured man's imagination as has the tiger. To me a wild tiger symbolizes freedom. Already our own freedom is becoming more and more relative as increased regimentation is required to control our growing population. If we allow the tiger to disappear, a part of ourselves may be lost forever. Nicholas Courtney has admirably demonstrated our compelling fascination for this beautiful creature by tracing it through history, art, literature, legend and religion. The tiger has long been the ultimate big game trophy, now at the eleventh hour we are striving desperately to save it.

I know well the attraction of this biggest and most beautiful of the cats, for it led me to India twenty years ago. I have had the extremely good fortune to spend most of the intervening period in tiger country. For the last eight years I have lived continuously in the heart of one of the best areas of tiger habitat left in Asia — the Royal Chitawan National Park in the lowlands of Nepal.

I would like to take this opportunity to say something about the problems of conserving an animal like the tiger. In order to effectively manage the reserves which have been set aside for this purpose, it is necessary to understand the basic aspects of tiger behaviour and to determine its habitat requirements. Despite man's long association with this super predator, it is only very recently that we have begun to acquire that knowledge.

Essentially solitary and mostly nocturnal, the tiger is a cautious and secretive hunter of large prey, at home only in areas where reed beds and forest provide sufficient cover. As can be imagined it is an exceedingly difficult subject for scientific study. Direct observations are limited. It has been necessary to rely on a variety of different but complementary methods to gather data concerning tiger behaviour. For example, the identification of individual tigers from distinctive features of their tracks, or 'pug marks', a study of the various signs which these cats use to mark their environment, and radiotelemetry all facilitate keeping track of particular tigers over sufficiently long periods of time to begin to understand what they are doing. Despite the difficulties involved, a few studies of different aspects of tiger behaviour have been completed and others continue.

A master predator, the tiger is at the apex of the food pyramid. In order to preserve the tiger it is necessary to preserve the entire ecosystem of which it is a part. Moreover, the tiger is a sensitive index of the condition of its environment. It will not remain long if the habitat degrades markedly, through loss of prey species, destruction of vegetation cover, or excessive human disturbance. On the other hand, a good tiger population reflects a healthy ecosystem.

As the result of 'Operation Tiger' launched in 1972, no fewer than sixteen special tiger reserves have been created in India, Nepal, Bhutan and Bangladesh. Other Asian countries also have taken steps to conserve tigers within their boundaries. A lot has been achieved. I have seen the results first hand at many locations in south Asia. Habitat quality has been improved through the professional management of reserves, exploitation has been stopped in core areas, and buffer zones have been created to accommodate some human needs while at the same time providing more space for the tigers. Those responsible for these accomplishments deserve our sincere gratitude. Nevertheless, we have not yet 'saved' the tiger. Statistics which appear to demonstrate large increases in the number of tigers in these reserves during a short period must be regarded with caution, and certainly should not lull us into complacency.

Research has determined that tigers are territorial animals. Resident males maintain relatively large territories including within them the smaller ones of usually two or more breeding females. The point to make is that territorial behaviour limits the amount of space available. Of course there is some flexibility, but at the same time, given a particular ecological situation, there is a point beyond which territories cannot be further compressed. Unless a 'vacancy' occurs locally through the loss of a resident adult territory holder, young tigers, that become independent at close to two years of age, must move out. They may move right out to the periphery, where they occupy areas of marginal habitat. This characteristically happens in the case of young males, among whom there is heavy attrition and a high turnover rate due to increased contact with man and other risks of living at the edge. Other young tigers may lead a transient existence, moving from one place to the next as they probe for space to establish a territory.

What all this means is that even given very high reproduction, the tiger population effectively protected may remain small if the reserve is too limited in size and no suitable habitat exists beyond it. Most reserves are too small, for the simple reason that humans had destroyed most of the tiger habitat before conservation came into the picture. Even when adjacent forest areas exist which might be used to expand reserves, the pressure of ever-expanding human needs often makes this difficult for political reasons. Nevertheless, there are heartening examples of where this has been achieved. Nepal's Royal Chitawan National Park, created in 1973, was expanded from 210 to 360 square miles in 1976, and a further extension is planned soon. But even this may be too small if the adjacent forest disappears.

So long as surrounding forest areas remain, it can be argued that the size of the reserve is not so critical so long as it serves as a breeding centre from which tigers can disperse beyond. But what happens when the adjacent forested tracks are destroyed, or so modified as to be useless, and the tiger reserve becomes an island in a sea of human activity, with a breeding population too small to ensure adequate genetical variability? And this is certainly the predictable result if man's population continues to grow at anything like the present rate.

It is therefore imperative that tiger reserves be expanded in size to whatever extent is humanly possible before it is too late. No conservation programme will succeed without the support of the local people. Buffer areas are essential to accommodate some human needs and at the same time to provide at least marginal habitat for dispersing tigers. Finally, wherever there remain corridors which link different reserves and sanctuaries these must be preserved at all costs to permit migration and genetic interchange.

CHARLES MCDOUGAL
Tiger Tops Jungle Lodge
Royal Chitawan National Park, Nepal

1

Tygre: A fierce beast of the leonine kind
Johnson

Late afternoon on a hot day in the vast forest covering the rugged sandstone of the Himalayan foothills, the air is drowsy with heat. Silence, save for the steady drone of bees. Only the sun's rays filter through the thick canopy of the trees.

Above, vultures circle and soar majestically, they scan the great stretches of sal forest with bamboo thickets below. Effortlessly they glide high above the numerous jungle-clad ridges and watercourses, cut deep by torrents over countless monsoon seasons. But the rains are months away and the torrent beds are dry except for the occasional shaded pool.

At one such pool a tiger is lying up (plate 1). A faint breeze stirs the bushes above, making shadows dance across the beautiful striped body. He lies sprawled on a smooth rock, head stretched between paws, body half submerged in the limpid water. He is dozing away the hours of heat secure in this cool retreat. Sometimes his ears twitch involuntarily, a quick flash of white against the cloud of worrying flies above his head. He stirs, yawns lazily, half closes his eyes and waits resignedly for dusk when once again he must set off in search of prey.

The afternoon gradually slips away. The heat goes out of the sun. The night-jar announces twilight with a monotonous *tonc-tonc* — the sound of a pebble hurled across ice.

The tiger, spurred to activity by hunger and the coolness of the evening, stretches his long rufous body, then crouches low as he drinks deeply to prepare for a strenuous night. His last kill, a wild pig, was finally abandoned to the forest scavengers three days ago. Since then the many miles travelled in his vast territory have produced nothing but frustration. He pads cautiously over the rocks, then, in a single leap, he is into the forest and away.

On the plateau above and some distance from the recumbent tiger, a sambar stag is standing motionless. His dark brown hide and massive three-tined horns make him invisible against the thick undergrowth. Alert and wary, he listens for sounds that suggest danger: the alarm calls of other deer, the agitated scream of a peacock or the harsh guttural cry of a langur monkey. Encouraged by hearing only the natural sounds of the forest, the buck ventures slightly away from the trees to browse the dry grass and stunted bushes. Every few seconds he stops to listen, ears swivelling like radar scanners, ever watchful, ever ready to take off at the first sign of danger.

The tiger steals through the undergrowth to a broad forest road, the baked clay deeply rutted from the huge wheels of bullock carts. He crouches low, pausing for a moment to decide which part of his territory to hunt. He is aware that his abortive wanderings of the night before will have alerted his prey so he must change his hunting ground tonight. The tiger lopes off, silently, muscles rippling, claws sheathed, moving with such precision that near fore- and off hind-legs seem as one. His great head, jaws parted and carried low, sways from side to side with the fluid movement of his body. The tip of his long tail is curled upwards. The ridge of prodigious muscles on nape and withers is accentuated as he glides over the ground. Despite his great weight only faint impressions, pug marks, are left in the hard earth to show that he has passed, so carefully does he place his paws on the ground.

A man is walking down the same path. Although still a long way off, the tiger can hear the steady beat of two feet which he easily identifies. Instantly he backs into a gully, freezes in a crouched position and waits for the familiar silhouette to pass. This would make easy prey were he interested, but, like the majority of his race, he is not a man-eater; although hungry, instinct tells him to leave man well alone. As the footsteps fade into the night the tiger sets off again on his search (plate 2).

When the pale moon emerges from behind the mountains, it lights the forest, casting eerie stripes of light and shade onto the path, black and yellow like the tiger who is stealthily moving towards the plateau. He stops every now and then to glance at the black shapes of monkeys asleep in the trees, checking that they are quite still. The forest floor is alive with small nocturnal mammals but they will not give the tiger away.

Through the intricate pattern of jungle paths, dry nullahs and fire-breaks, the tiger reaches the plateau. He has covered at least ten miles in three hours since leaving his resting place. Every step is now crucial as he skirts round the edge of the flat lands, listening, watching. His hunch is right, his instinct and experience pay off, as he picks up the barely audible sound of the crunch of dried leaves carried on the faint night breeze: the noise of a sambar stag feeding.

It takes a full fifteen minutes for the tiger to ease forward far enough to see his prey. He crouches low, belly a fraction above the ground, each step minutely calculated: here a dry leaf avoided, there a brittle twig. His hind feet fit exactly the safe spot vacated by the fore; the dry grass parts noiselessly as he inches his way towards his prey.

The stag, majestic in the pale moonlight, now totally confident, stands high on his hind legs to browse the tops of a zizyphus bush. The tiger watches as the long tongue curls round the dead leaves. Satisfied with the approach, he weighs up the final plan of attack. He rises off his haunches slightly, stretching his neck as if focusing. The stag drops down on all fours and begins to chew the dry leaves. He is standing with his back to the danger, slightly at an angle. This position is perfect for the tiger, who is, after all, a seasoned killer. Every muscle is taut, every sinew strained. The attack comes in an explosion of unleashed power. In just three long strides and in less than a second the tiger is onto the sambar; claws splayed, tail erect, he lands square on the stag's back. The claws sink deep and blood flows. The startled *pook*, the sambar's cry of alarm, is stifled as sharp canines sink into the nape of the neck. The stag collapses from the sheer weight of its killer. As they crash to the ground, an antler, totally ineffective against such a mighty killing machine, splinters. The tiger deftly avoids the jagged stump then strikes the *coup de grâce*, seizing the throat and remaining motionless until all life is suffocated.

Without pausing for rest, the tiger drags the carcass under cover of the trees, unconcerned by its weight (plate 3). Once the prey is hidden, the tiger goes off to drink. He does not care who hears him now as he crashes through the undergrowth to a pool below. He drinks, lapping the cool water with his tongue. He is now ready to eat. Bounding back to his meal, he ignores the shrieks of alarm that upset the once sleeping forest.

The tiger rolls his lips back into a dreadful grimace to bare razor-sharp incisor teeth. He gnaws a patch of hair from the haunch then rasps the skin away with his rough tongue. He bites the still warm flesh into a pulp as he tears it open against his forepaws. The tiger works steadily until the carcass is half skinned.

Finally he is ready to feed. Deciding to start with the offal, he forces his head right into the carcass and takes the liver gently in his teeth. As he pulls, intestines follow; another bite and the kidneys come away.

He plunges his head in again, and draws out the heart taking care not to rupture the rumen, for if broken it will ruin the flesh. The tiger eats hungrily, swallowing every piece of the innards before tearing at the flesh on the haunches. Each bone is picked clean before another is started, every morsel of flesh stripped off by that rough tongue. His immediate hunger satisfied, he pads round the kill, stretches, and then heads off towards the pool to drink, belching loudly.

Blood colours the water as the tiger laps thirstily. Resting beside the pool, he begins to clean himself, licking the sticky fur about his forequarters. Then his head and ears, the beginnings of a ruff about his face, and finally his whiskers are cleaned by his paws. It is just one a.m. and there is still plenty more time to feed. He dozes fitfully disturbed only by the rumblings in his stomach, caused by the digestion of the unchewed hunks of meat.

Later the tiger returns to his kill to find a pair of jackals feeding. He gives a fierce *woof* and they disappear instantly, thankful for their lives.

At last, the raucous cry of a peafowl announces dawn. Grey light creeps through the forest. The tiger has had a full meal, at least a third of the edible part of the sambar. However, he is not accommodating and does not wish to share his meal with other carnivores so he drags his prize further into the forest, hiding it beneath some low sweeping branches.

Satiated, the tiger saunters over to a simal tree and, standing on his hind-legs scores the bark into deep fissures to cleanse his claws of the little pieces of meat that, rotted, would turn his feet sceptic (plate 6).

The forest is now awake, but somehow all the inhabitants know that the tiger who is passing below is gorged and presents no threat. Even the monkeys in the trees hardly leave off their games.

Without giving his kill another thought the tiger pads off to find a new place to lie up against the heat of the day (plate 5). He chooses a patch of damp sand by a pool under some overhanging rocks, cool and well shaded, the banks covered with the graceful foliage of maidenhair fern.

He drinks briefly, gives out a contented roar, then crawls into his chosen position, secure and content that the sambar will last for two, possibly three nights. Two days' respite before he has to go hunting again.

1   Tiger musing on a rock

2 · The prowl

3   The tiger drags his kill into the undergrowth

4   The sensitivity of the tiger's whiskers

5   Hunger satisfied for one day

6   Tiger cleaning his claws on the bark of a tree in the Royal Chitawan National Park, Nepal

2

There are no tigers in Africa
Pax Britannica

A tiger sleeping off a meal is indistinguishable from his surroundings, his vivid stripes and glossy coat blend with the confusion of tangled branches, shafts of sunlight, shadow and tall dead grass. His camouflage consists of a series of broken, irregular stripes over back and flanks and a body of an orange-red hue which fades to tawny yellow, gradually merging into white about the belly and chest. Horizontal bars on the limbs, a black striped tail and a speckled and short lined face help to confuse the eye most effectively.

This camouflage is versatile. Even a tiger basking half out of the water looks like a boulder, his outline becoming indistinct in the dazzling sunshine. In the bamboo thickets the tiger merges with the yellow stems and his black stripes look like shadows cast by the slim leaves; in the dry deciduous forests he blends with the brownish-yellow foliage and slanting shadows that criss-cross the forest floor. Grassland, jungle, forest and tiger blur and blend in endless permutations, the single mass broken up into stripes, spots and shadows. But not for the tiger the open monochrome savanna which so suits the duller tawny lion.

Effective camouflage not only protects the tiger from his enemies when he is comatose, but also conceals the tiger from his prey. At dusk or at night, the usual hunting times of the tiger, the stripes break up the bold outline turning the predator into a mere grey shadow.

It would seem likely that the forebears of the tiger had always inhabited areas of thick forest or jungle since the colouration of their coats seems so exceptionally well suited to such surroundings. But the generally accepted theory is that the tiger originated — stripes and all – in the monochrome barren wastes of northern Asia and that in the time of the Pleistocene glacial advances it was forced to follow its prey southwards and migrate down through central Asia and China into south-east Asia, Indonesia and on to Bali, fanning out into the whole subcontinent except for Sri Lanka. (There are no tigers in Sri Lanka, only leopards. The leopard must have come while there was still a landbridge between the subcontinent and the island but the tiger must have reached the south after this bridge had disappeared and when the gap was too wide for him to swim across.)

I do not hold with this theory because it seems to me most unlikely that the tiger would possess such versatile striped camou-flage if it had begun life in an area of bleak, sandy scrubland. Instead I think that the animal forced south by the ice was a form of cave lion and that over the centuries, this cave lion adapted a dull yellow coat in open dry savannah, a spotted leopard skin in dry tropical areas and a splendid set of tiger stripes in areas of wet variegated jungle. When the climate altered yet again and the ice-cap retreated from central Asia and Manchuria and the forests re-established themselves, then this striped tiger from the jungle moved north after its prey into the new ice-free areas.

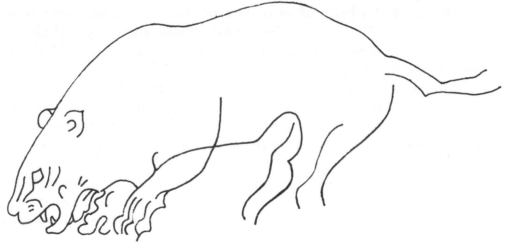

Fig. 1   Cave lion engraved on stone slab, La Marche, France

The tiger, the lion and the leopard are all large cats, genus *Panthera*, so named because of their unique ability to roar due to a flexible attachment of the larynx. The cave lion was also of the genus *Panthera*; moreover, the fossil remains of cave lion, leopard, lion and tiger are skeletally remarkably similar save for the skull, which in the tiger is slightly shorter and somewhat more vaulted (plate 9). There is of course no record of skin type, fur, colour or stripes with any skeletal remains to prove these theories either way. But it seems

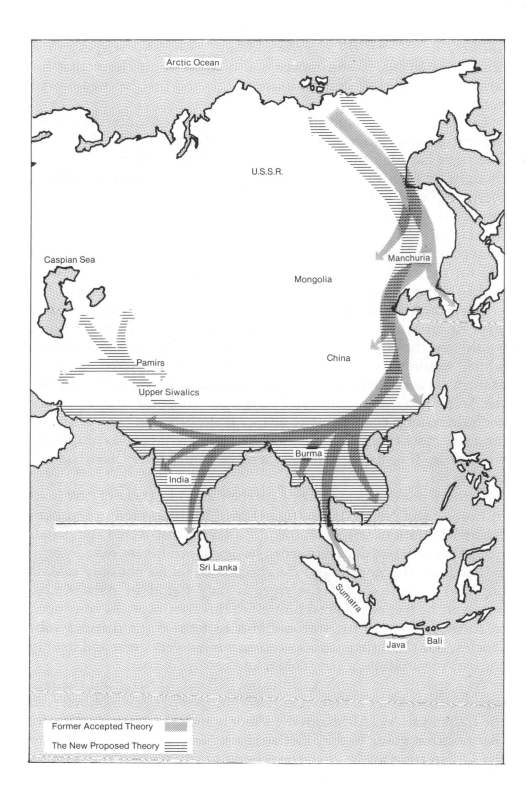

Fig. 2   Dispersal of the tiger

unlikely to me that the tiger would have gained his stripes in the central Asian plains and moved south. I prefer to think that his stripes came from adaptation to the jungle and that he then moved north.

Considering the migration in this way answers questions about the texture and colour of the tiger's pelt. But what of its thickness? The tiger has long fur, particularly the new-born cubs, and this is thought by some to be a hangover from his Siberian origins. What, these people say, would the tiger want with such thick fur in tropical jungle? But just as this thick coat can be uncomfortable in the heat of the day, although a tiger can usually find a shady or damp place to keep cool, it is invaluable during the extreme cold at night, especially for the cubs. I believe the thick fur was designed for the cold nights in Asian jungle rather than the snows of the frozen north.

Then there are those who say that the tiger has developed an extra layer of fat and longer fur to combat icy Siberian winters. But I would say the tiger developed these attributes as he moved north which would explain why the animal in snow-covered northern Manchuria and Siberia still has a rufous coat and not a white one like the Arctic foxes, snow hares and partridges – it is just that he has not been there long enough yet to adapt. If the Siberian tiger is spared for a few more thousand years perhaps he too will have a completely white coat. If he had originated there, he would surely have had one by now.

Perhaps one day cave drawings of the tiger, like those of cave lions in Europe and North Africa (fig. 1), will be discovered in southern Asia with glorious stripes on them. If they are discovered and dated, maybe we will one day learn when he developed his stripes.

The lion, the leopard and the cheetah are found not only in Asia but also in Africa. But the tiger is only found in Asia. Once, however, he had established himself in this continent, he continued to further adapt to his surroundings to form eight distinct sub-species, but the difference between each is not very great and mainly consists of variation in size, colour and texture of coat.

As a species the tiger's Latin name is *Panthera tigris* and the race type for the species is known as *Panthera tigris tigris*, which refers to the Indian variety. Although the senior branch, he is not the largest, that position going to the Siberian tiger. Nevertheless to the hunter the Indian tiger was quite large enough to be a worthy trophy. Size was all important and so there are many records extant of the length of tigers shot. Early measurements were taken 'over curves', that is, the tape measure followed the curves of the body which of course added several extra inches to the real length. Later a more accurate

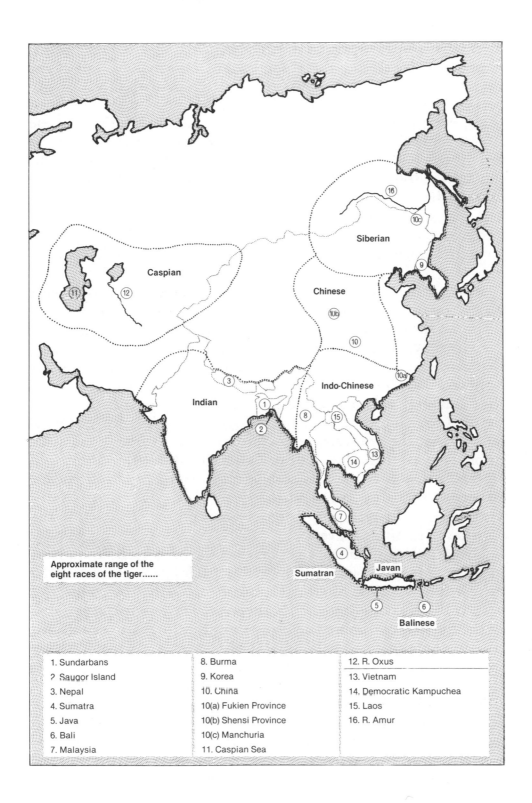

Approximate range of the eight races of the tiger......

1. Sundarbans	8. Burma	12. R. Oxus
2. Saugor Island	9. Korea	13. Vietnam
3. Nepal	10. China	14. Democratic Kampuchea
4. Sumatra	10(a) Fukien Province	15. Laos
5. Java	10(b) Shensi Province	16. R. Amur
6. Bali	10(c) Manchuria	
7. Malaysia	11. Caspian Sea	

Fig. 3   Approximate world range of the tiger

method was introduced and the tiger was measured 'between pegs'. A peg was driven into the ground at the nose and the tail of the stretched out dead tiger, the corpse was removed and the distance between pegs was measured. The largest Indian male, 'between pegs', ever recorded, was eleven feet five-and-a-half inches and the largest female measured a foot shorter. The largest recorded tiger weight was 570 pounds and the heaviest tigress was 360 pounds. An Indian tiger of eleven feet four-and-a-half inches was shot in Nepal and another weighing 635 pounds measured ten feet nine inches. These are extreme figures, the average size of the Indian tiger is nine feet six inches, the tigress nearly a foot shorter, the average weight for the male being 400 to 450 pounds, the female about 100 pounds lighter.

Panthera tigris tigris, the Indian tiger, is capable of living in a wide variety of habitats, from the *terai* to the wet Sundarbans, for he adapts well. The *terai* are those vast savannas about the foothills of the Himalaya where the land is flat with marsh and ponds, where elephant grass with tall whispery stems is so dense that even its namesake has difficulty in forcing a way through. Tall trees with wide canopies are interspersed haphazardly throughout. In spring the picture changes dramatically. Villagers burn the grass before the rains so that the green shoots can force their way through the black stubble to feed their domestic cattle. But this also attracts deer, wild pig and other prey animals accompanied by their ever-attendant predators, probably including the tiger. It is good tiger country with numerous rivers, deep gorges below and the sanctuary of the Himalayan foothills above.

The same sub-species of tiger inhabits the hard lands of southern and central India. These were the traditional hunting grounds of the British Raj, all close to army encampments. This is a country of stony hills, dry table-lands and burnt earth. The jungle is sparse save for the thickets of bamboo and date palms. But there are deep shaded ravines, some that still hold water in the dry season. Here it is very hot, and the tiger's coat is so thin it seems that his stripes have been painted on.

North-west to the Sundarbans, there is an even greater contrast of environment. For 200 miles these saline swamps and islands stretch across the Ganges delta. Here the tiger, sometimes called the Sundarbans or Bengal tiger, leads a semi-aquatic life in mangrove swamps. He, too, has adapted to his environment possessing a lighter body, smaller head and thinner tapering tail than others of the same sub-species. His is inhospitable country, where an impenetrable tangle of undergrowth covers the small islands and the land is constantly underwater from floods and high tides. Even the intricate network of streams are saline, forcing the tiger to drink brackish water unless he is fortunate enough to find a rain puddle.

The Indo-Chinese or Malay tiger is named after the legendary hunter turned conservationist, Jim Corbett. *Panthera tigris corbetti* inhabits the jungles of south-east Asia, from the sodden rain forests of Assam right through to Vietnam, up to, and now including, southern China and below to the Malay peninsula. This species is slightly smaller, the average length being around eight foot three inches which makes it the size of a nearly full-grown Indian tiger cub. It is generally thought that the hotter the climate the smaller the species, as the increased ratio of weight to evaporation surface — the skin — helps to dissipate body heat.

Mind makes the man.

Fig. 4   Arms of Lord Milverton with the Malay tiger, *Panthera tigris corbetti*, acting as supporters and crest

Sumatra has a species of its own, *Panthera tigris sumatrae*. Like the Indian tiger, his territory is diverse, ranging from the rain forests in the centre of the island to the wide savannas and mangrove swamps towards the coast. He is small like *Panthera tigris corbetti* but slightly darker. The Javan tiger, *Panthera tigris sondaica*, is even smaller and very dark as his stripes are closer together. *Panthera tigris balica*, the Bali tiger, the smallest of the species, used to inhabit the rain forests of the island and is now almost certainly extinct.

The tiger thrives equally well in a climate as extreme as China, the home of *Panthera tigris amoyensis*. There he inhabits the spruce forests in the north around the Shansi Province, the south and east steep foothills and the marshy plains as far as the Fulkien Province and the

Yangstze river, the border of the Indo-China tiger's territory.

This tiger's coat is thick and woolly to withstand the severe Chinese winters. It makes him look large but he is in fact only about the same size as his Indian neighbour. By comparison his coat is slightly paler and less richly striped, but with a much bushier tail.

It is not only the thick, long fur and undercoat, and the extra layer of fat that makes the Siberian tiger, *Panthera tigris altaica*, look huge. His skeleton is larger and he has been known to measure thirteen feet 'between pegs', but the average is nearer eleven feet, weighing 650 pounds. Beneath the dense fur is a powerfully-built animal with a massive head and a fine ruff about his cheeks and throat. Like his neighbour, his coat is paler than those of the southern sub-species. The Siberian tiger, occasionally called the Amur tiger or the Manchurian tiger, formerly commanded a vast range throughout Russian and Chinese Manchuria and all Korea. Now he is confined to the coniferous forests around the River Arun and its tributaries.

Once tigers were common below the snow line of Mount Ararat in eastern Turkey. The shores of the Caspian Sea were also their domain. The great reed beds and marshes of the Oxus river held tigers, as did the foothills of the Pamir range and northern Iran. The Caspian tiger, *Panthera tigris virgata*, has now gone forever. When he was alive he ranked second only to the Siberian tiger in size and was thick-set and powerful, with a long coat to cope with the snows.

All that vast and varied country used to belong to the undisputed animal king of the largest continent. But he has been deposed by man, his lands violated and his species slaughtered with such ruthless determination that there are now few tigers left.

3
Tiggers don't climb trees
A.A. Milne

The tiger lives within a clearly defined home range, a territorial area which must be large enough to provide him with adequate food, water and shelter. He will not share this territory with another tiger but it will always encompass at least one, and probably more, tigress's home range. Contact is made with female tigers, even outside the mating season, but not usually with other males.

The inner sanctuary of the home range is sacred and is defended against all intruders. This defence is not usually a vicious tooth and claw affair as both tigers, being hunting animals, cannot afford to be wounded. Instead the tiger will avoid a confrontation by marking his home range with various signs which warn other males to keep away.

Periodically the tiger patrols his territory leaving certain marks to advertise that his home range is occupied. These also attract a mate. On his rounds the tiger sprays a particularly pungent pale yellow liquid onto bushes every half mile or so. The tigress's spray is less strong than the male's but both last for days, sometimes weeks if not washed away by the rains. Scrape marks, often with droppings, are another territorial sign. Sometimes just the droppings indicate a home range, but more often it is a combination of all three. When a home range falls vacant for any reason it is quickly filled by another tiger.

Roaring can be another form of claiming territorial ownership but is seldom used since, unlike the lion, the tiger is not a noisy animal. When roaring does occur, it is a remarkably efficient deterrent to trespassers, as one tiger can gauge the size and strength of another by the volume of sound. On a still night in the jungle the terrifying *aa—oonn* will reverberate for a radius of at least two miles. The first call is shortly followed by an explosive *oo—oo—oongh*.

The tigress also roars or gives a mixture of a roar and a moan, when she is on heat. A calling tigress seldom has to wait long before she is answered but while she waits she works herself up into a frenzy of frustrated fury and becomes a very dangerous animal indeed. The tiger that answers her call is likely to be the resident male of her home range but occasionally a neighbour or transient tiger moves in. Whoever feels he is the possessor becomes very protective towards his mate and is not to be thwarted with impunity.

When the tigress is courted by more than one tiger the fight that ensues is serious, although rarely to the death as the vanquished is given ample opportunity to back off. One eye-witness reported that he decided to climb a tree when he heard a tigress call rather too close to him for comfort.[1] It was a prudent move as her call was answered by one tiger, then moments later by another two. The tigress walked out into the glade, below the witness, and began to call to all three.

The first tiger walked out of the jungle, stopped and gazed at the tigress. She laid her ears back and dropped to a prone position on the grass, flicking her tail to one side. The tiger gave a deep-seated, hollow *grr-aounch* and advanced towards her. Suddenly, from a thicket, there was a flash of black and red flying through the air, as another male, nearly the size of the first one, leapt for his rival. The first sprang nimbly aside, snarling and growling with rage. These two glowered at each other, ears flat, crouching, their tails lashing furiously. The young tigress sat, peacefully cleaning her fur while the rivals fought and the jungle reverberated with the sound of their growls and roars. After a few minutes the tigress stood up and walked to the shade of a tree, raised herself onto her haunches and stared wistfully at a thicket, her tail flicking wildly. The third tiger merely watched her and the combatants, totally unconcerned.

The fight continued for another five minutes and by this time both tigers were bleeding freely. They wrestled savagely, standing on their hind-legs, biting and clawing, roaring angrily and snarling. They fell to the ground, scuffling. Suddenly one tiger tore the other's neck open with its claws, making a vicious wound. The wounded tiger limped away to the victor's growls, but he too was badly wounded with weals over body and head. Presently he threw himself on the grass, wiped the blood from his face and went to claim his sleek young tigress. She rose, glanced towards the thicket, then went to her champion. He came to within five paces of her when the third tiger sprang. The injured tiger attacked the usurper but was soon chased away to the edge of the jungle where he waited and watched. The tigress then threw herself onto the grass and rolled onto her back until the final victor came to claim his prize. They played for a while then she sprang up and bounded swiftly into the jungle. He followed at breakneck speed. Apparently the two original suitors were neighbours, the first an adult, the second a cub, most likely his, while the third was an interloper searching for a territory of his own.

There are few accounts of tiger courtship and mating in the wild. Even the great naturalists who lived for years in tiger country have only caught a glimpse of the act or found signs after the event. Native peoples, well aware of the dangers of being around courting tigers, always give them a wide berth for there are many stories of men spending nights in trees having incurred their displeasure.

However, it is possible to piece together a picture of the act from fragmented sources backed up by observations in a zoo. After the tigress's mating call has been answered, the tiger will apear and stand quite still before her. Courtship begins with the tigress rubbing her body down the side of her mate. She then 'kisses' him, rubbing his muzzle and biting him gently on the neck. Sometimes the courtship can be rough:

> with blazing eyes, ears laid back and tail twitching, her attitude for the moment was anything but that of a loving wife. Waiting 'till the tiger was within a few paces, she sprang towards him as if bent on his annihilation, lifted a forepaw, and gently patted him on the side of the face. Then she raised her head and obviously kissed him.[2]

After a mock chase the tigress squats in a prone position and the tiger straddles her, barely touching her back (plate 36). Copulation is swift, between fifteen and twenty-five seconds. The tigress moans with a deep *oaar oaaa*. The tiger grasps the folds of her neck firmly, but carefully, with his teeth, then squeals with a high pitched metallic *aee oaaa* that becomes an *aee aee*. At that moment the tigress whips round and her mate has to spring back sharply to avoid her hefty swipe. They face each other, rise on their haunches and spar wildly, grunting and snarling so that both parties are sometimes quite badly injured . Her show of strength over, the tigress rolls onto her back, exhausted, paws flopping in the air.

The swiftness of copulation is more than compensated for by the tiger's incredible ability to carry on mating within a few minutes of the first act and continue for several days. It is not uncommon for couples to copulate over a hundred times during a four day period. After mating, the tiger will leave the tigress. If their home ranges overlap, which is likely, they will meet briefly and possibly share a kill but the tiger will take no further interest in her, or in the cubs when they are born, until she comes on heat again.

To raise cubs from birth to a time when they are fully independent is a daunting task that can take up to two-and-a-half years. The gestation period is short, around fifteen weeks, and only in the last two weeks does her pregnancy affect her. Then she is at her most vulnerable, not being able to hunt easily. The cubs are born in a secluded spot: a trampled down patch of grass, a thick bush or in the shelter of a rock. Not surprisingly, the cubs are small after such a short gestation period, and weigh between two-and-a-half and three pounds. The litter usually consists of two or three cubs although some dead tigresses, when examined, were carrying as many as seven foetuses and sightings of a tigress accompanied by five cubs have been recorded but are not common.

The cubs are born blind. The membrane over their eyes does not break for several days and even then they remain fairly myopic for a few weeks which keeps them from straying when the mother is away hunting. The tigress suckles her young for up to six months, but after three months she will offer them small pieces of chewed meat in the lair from her kills.

The tigress is an excellent mother, licking her cubs spotlessly clean and keeping the 'nursery' immaculate. She is most protective towards her cubs, defending them against all intruders, if necessary to the death. If she suspects that the secrecy of the lair has been violated, or if she is disturbed in any way, she will carry her cubs one by one to a new hide-out. Taking each cub's head into her mouth in turn (plate 37), she will move them with extreme caution, taking great care to cover her tracks by using stony paths and varying the times of her journeys.

Despite this maternal care, the mortality rate of cubs is high. As the tigress is the sole provider for herself and her cubs, she must leave her invariably noisy offspring for long periods when she goes hunting. When prey is scarce the cubs are at the mercy of other carnivores, not least other tigers, including their own father. Crocodiles have been known to snatch a cub when they were brought down to the river to drink.

Gradually the cubs are weaned onto a meat diet. At first the mother will bring the kill back to the lair for them to eat but when they are stronger she will take them to the kill, calling them with a series of low grunts. She cannot take them hunting with her until they are amenable to discipline as naturally all element of surprise would be lost if she were to be followed through the jungle by vociferous, gambolling cubs. Unlike the lioness, who always eats before the cubs, the tigress opens up a kill to enable her young to feed before satisfying her own hunger.

After six months, the tigress will begin to teach her cubs the basic skills of hunting. At that age the cubs are extremely active and playful like their domestic counterparts. They worry their mother, taking particular delight in stalking her tail as it flicks about when she is sleeping, a game rewarded by a firm cuff. At this age the males weigh around a hundred pounds, the females considerably less, although both are the same size at about six feet. The tigress leads the stalk while the cubs follow behind, imitating every move. They place their feet in exactly the same spot as their mother, sink to the ground or drop when she drops behind cover. She starts them off on easy prey: hares, peafowl, even small deer.

Once the cubs have mastered the stalk, their mother introduces them to the complexities of killing. As with all canivores, killing is instinctive and not something that is taught, although the tigress plays an important part in perfecting her cubs' skills. Often the cubs are slow to master their art which causes considerable suffering to the prey animal as they claw at haunches and sides before their mother can intervene with the *coup de grâce*. Such poor displays usually earn a severe blow from the instructress.

Cubs will be at least a year old before they can kill even the smallest animal, such as a young boar or chital fawn, efficiently. Sometimes two cubs together take on a tethered bullock or buffalo with eventual success. Once they master the lethal art, the cubs often slay for pleasure, frequently with the mother joining in to finish off the kill.

Another lesson on the cubs' curriculum is swimming. Swimming does not seem to be an innate characteristic as cubs are reluctant to even approach the water's edge. The tigress will lead the way, calling her young from the water with an encouraging purr. If they do not respond she will take each one in turn in her mouth and hold it under the water for a few seconds, then return it to the bank. This shock treatment seems to work well as the cubs are usually quite happy to swim the next day.

When the cubs are nearly full-grown, usually around eighteen to twenty months, the family breaks up. This is a gradual process which the tigress starts by leaving her offspring for a week at a time, slowly increasing the periods. If on her ramblings she finds a mate and becomes pregnant again, the tiger will certainly object to the presence of a nearly mature male cub. If game is short in the tigress's home range she will ease out her adult cubs.

Whatever the reason for their departure, the young adults will wander further and further afield in an attempt to find new unoccupied territories. They may travel great distances in order to find an empty home range with enough prey animals, water and shelter. Often they have to make do with inferior territories or intrude on one that is already occupied. A young tigress will not normally mate before she is three, even four years old, so she too, like her brothers, must find her own home range. With the ratio of three males to one female the sub-adult tigress's task of finding her own home range will be the easier. She will traverse the whole territory, often many times, until she finds a home range where she can slot in between two other females. The male, on the other hand, will have to start in the peripheral areas until he too can move into a vacant home range or take one over.

Under exceptional circumstances it has been known for a tiger or a tigress to be forced into ranges inhabited by the Asian lion, *Panthera leo persica*, which is the same genus as the tiger. Rare reports have been made of tigresses mating with lions in the wild and producing offspring known as ligers. When a tiger and a lioness mate, the cub is called a tigron. Unfortunately, like all animal hybrids, these young are themselves infertile. There has even been an account of the sighting of an animal though to be the cross between a tiger and a female panther. This particular specimen disappeared after seriously mauling the witness who described his attacker:

> its head and neck were purely those of a panther but the body, shoulders and neck ruff unmistakeably of a tiger – the black stripes being broad and long, though somewhat blurred rosettes, the stripes of the tiger being most prominent in the body. The animal was a male and measuring a little over eight feet.[3]

Tiger crosses in captivity have been common for centuries. One of the best known tigrons was Ranji who was bred by Prince Ranjitsinji of Nawangagar and presented by him to the Zoological Gardens in Regent's Park in 1928. Mr Frohawk was commissioned by *The Field* to sketch Ranji. He found him shy and said that:

> the hybrid favours the tiger rather than the lion in the shape of the body and head and it is particularly interesting to note that although the creature is a male, the mane is not larger than that possessed by some tigers and there is at most a small tuft at the end of the tail. The coat, however, is tawny and entirely lacks the reddish-orange hue characteristic of all tigers except those of the colder regions of central Asia. The stripes, nevertheless, although comparatively faint are clearly traceable and the lower parts of the body are whitish as in tigers.[4]

There has only been one record of a true albino tiger, one with a pale skin and pink eyes, although there have been many white or cream-coloured tigers seen over the last hundred years. The most famous are the white tigers of Rewa, which all have particularly attractive brownish-grey stripes on a white background with bluish eyes (plate 35). Their origins are particularly interesting. A white male was captured in the forests of Rewa in 1951 and the Maharajah of Rewa mated it with a normal-coloured tigress. She produced three perfectly ordinary litters. A tigress from the second litter was mated with her father, the white tiger, and produced four white cubs with pale blue eyes. The delighted maharajah rewarded the tigress, the white tiger and the cubs with residence at his summer palace at Govindgarh where they still live and breed. Many of the progeny have been given to zoos all over the world.

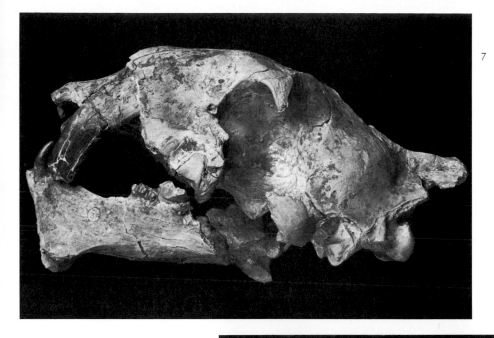

7 Skull of a hoplophoneus, one of the earliest sabre-tooth or stabbing cats, from the Oligocene epoch (38 million years ago). An early *Felidae,* this genus hunted slow-moving mammals like mammoths and mastodons and became extinct when their prey animals died out at the end of the Pleistocene epoch (2 million years ago). It is believed that they evolved, like all carnivores, from the *Miacids,* in the Eocene epoch (54 million years ago). Another cat form, *Dinictis,* dating from the Oligocene, is regarded as the likely ancestor of the modern tiger

8 Head of a cave lion from Dolní Věstoniče, Czechoslovakia, made of clay and powdered bone around 20,000 years ago.

9 Skull of *Panthera tigris tigris,* the Indian tiger

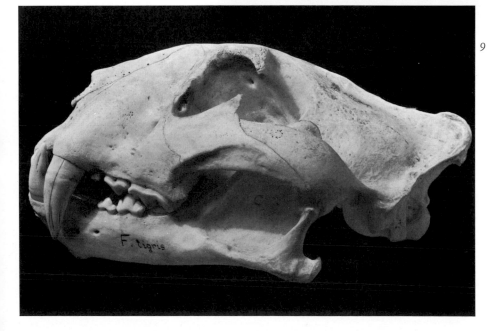

10   'Walking Tiger', bronze by A. L. Barye, circa 1840

11   Bronze statuette of a tigress with stripes made of copper. Mid Hellenistic period, 300-200 B.C.

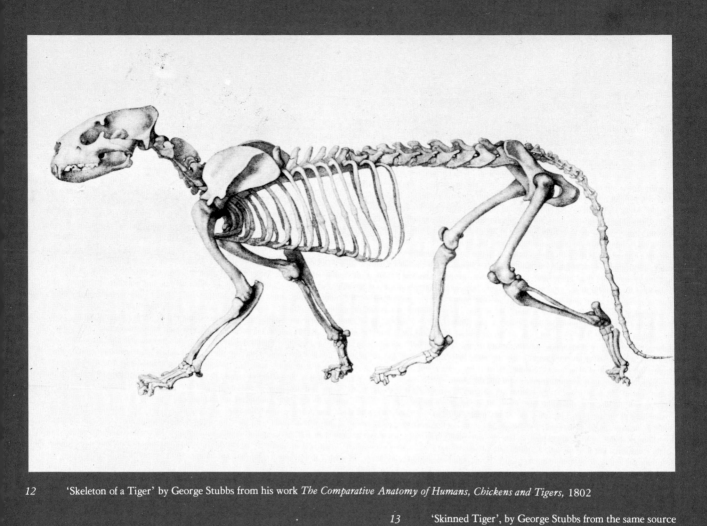

12   'Skeleton of a Tiger' by George Stubbs from his work *The Comparative Anatomy of Humans, Chickens and Tigers,* 1802

13   'Skinned Tiger', by George Stubbs from the same source

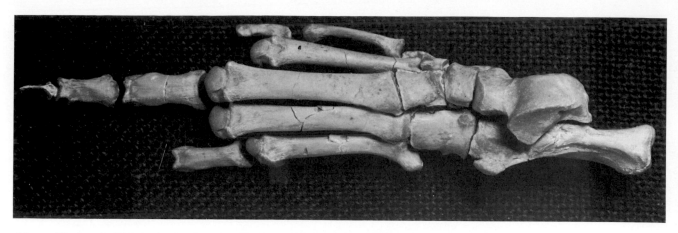

14   The foot of a *Dinictis,* showing the retractable claws which the modern tiger has inherited

15   A *waghnak.* This particularly unpleasant steel weapon (called after the Hindu word for a tiger claw, *waghnak),* was a favourite of its inventor Siviji, the founder of the Maratha Empire (seventeenth century) who tore out the entrails of the Mogul general, Atzul Khan, while embracing him

16(a)   The pug marks, or footprints, of a tiger stalking, where the back legs fall on the exact spot vacated by the front legs, leaving a single trail   16(b)   The pug marks of a tiger that is ambling along

4

A chaos of claws, fangs, torsos and backs
Delacroix

There is nothing wasted in the composition of the tiger, he is a totally functional animal. Each part of his anatomy is designed for maximum efficiency; every movement economical and every sense acute.

The exceptionally versatile nature of his subtle skin markings which enable him to remain camouflaged against such a wide variety of backgrounds has already been mentioned. His skeleton, too, is remarkable for the perfection of its mechanism for the bones are compact, dense and strong, protecting the digestive system. Like all carnivores, the stomach is simple; the intestines, in particular the colon and caecum or appendix, are short giving him quicker digestion. Often the liver is covered with small lobes — legend dictates that the number of lobes will correspond with the age of the tiger in years. This is, however, a fallacy as some cubs have many lobes while some adult tigers have none at all.

In Malaysia and China it has been a common belief for centuries that the courage and strength of a tiger are passed on to those who eat his liver or flesh, whereas the fat has always been popular in India as a tonic for rheumatism. Today this habit of eating tiger meat has been extended to the United States of America and to parts of Europe, where one successful German butcher exports the meat all over the world. Do his clientele, too, believe they will inherit the qualities of the tiger by eating his body? In Taiwan they drink tiger bone wine in the belief it will give strength and courage. At leat two hundred tiger skeletons a year are exported from Thailand and Indonesia to make 100,000 bottles of wine, which hardly satisfies the market demand. One particular bone, the clavicle, which is embedded in the muscle of the shoulder, used to be much sought after as an amulet or charm against evil. The Chinese believed that the tiger derived his power from this rudimentary bone, the small, slim *wei*. As it was supposed to retain its magic power for ever it was highly prized, ensuring respect from both humans and animals for the new owner.

Another charm against evil was the tiger's claw. Old tiger hunters often complained that the claws were 'apt to vanish, of course nobody knew how. But these claws were hung round children's necks as charms against all sorts of evil.'[1] In the Victorian and Edwardian eras they were often used in jewellery, simply mounted with a band of gold or sometimes as more ornate pieces (plate 61).

Like many members of the cat family the tiger can retract his claws, a trait inherited from their common ancestor, *Dinictis* (plate 14). The last toe bones, which carry the claws, are held back by elastic ligaments. The claws are only extended for seizing prey, fighting, killing or cleaning, when the muscle on the leg contracts and the attached tendons pull the last toe bones of the foot forward. The ligaments stretch as the claws emerge from the sheath.

A tiger will always sheath his claws in a fold of skin, except when startled, wounded or frightened, so they do not become blunted when moving over the hard ground. The imprint he leaves is called a pug mark and there are many experts who can recognize individual tigers by these marks and discover everything about them as clearly as if they were looking at the animal. A good tracker can tell the size of the tiger by the depth and indentation of the pug mark. At birth cubs have the same sized feet, but after three months the male's are almost half as large again as the female's, a difference which remains throughout life. Cubs' pug marks are disproportionately large compared with their weight and so are consequently shallow. A full-grown male may leave a heavy indentation as long as six inches. An old tiger will have splayed or cracked feet and these will show in the pug marks just as extended claw marks will indicate a wounded or frightened animal. The positioning of the pug marks tells the expert exactly what the tiger was doing and how fast he was moving.

One of the most unusual aspects of the tiger is the way he walks. When he is ambling about or stalking both near-side legs move together followed by both off-side legs, like a camel or a bear. Here the pug marks are in a straight line, the fore pug marks often being covered by those of the back feet when stalking (plate 16(a)) or even two to four inches in front when moving faster (plate 16 (b)). This unusual gait for a member of the cat family gives the tiger a rolling movement when he is going very slowly. When the pace quickens to a fast walk he reverts to type and moves his legs alternately like other quadrupeds. As he increases his speed to a run the tiger has only one leg on the ground at a time, as if cantering (plate 31), and finally when he springs he launches himself with incredible power from his hind-legs leaping a distance of anything up to thirty feet before landing on his fore-legs. The hind-legs then come in front of the fore-legs by a few inches ready to spring again. This magnificent fluidity of motion can only really be caught by a cine-camera (plate 38).

At the moment when the tiger finally springs onto his prey his tail is arched like a bow with the tip bent downwards. Like other members of the cat family, the tiger shows his moods and feelings through tail movements. When he is asleep or basking in the sun, the tip will flick involuntarily. When excited, the tail twitches from side to side, accelerating to a furious lashing as he gets angrier. His tail will shoot up in the air when tense or excited, particularly when stalking.

These tail movements uusually occur in conjunction with whisker oscillation for the whiskers, too, betray the tiger's mood. Normally a placid animal, the tiger's whiskers slant lazily downwards but the moment he is aroused, they shoot upwards, bristling with fury. The whiskers are extremely sensitive, the merest brush with an object on a pitch black night will be picked up and relayed from the tip, as fine as human hair, through the thick bristle base to the nerve system and brain. A remarkable photograph, taken by F. W. Champion, of a tiger lifting his paw after his whiskers had picked up a thin trip wire, illustrates just how sensitive they are (plate 4).

In many countries a tiger's whiskers, ground into a powder, is believed to be lethal. In Indo-China a single whisker threaded into a bamboo shoot is thought to cause internal bleeding and ensure a slow death. In China ground-up tiger whiskers are considered to be a cure for toothache. The Indonesians hope that they have the power to cure impotency.

The inside of the tiger's mouth is often portrayed as red whereas it is in fact a dull pinkish-grey. His long tongue is covered with papillæ, rough nodules that will strip flesh from a bone, clean the dirtiest fur or cleanse a wound. There is some question as to whether the tiger has a sense of taste, but for what other reason would he tackle a porcupine, with its obvious risks, if he did not hanker for its flavour? Wild boar is another favourite but highly risky prey, with its solid weight and lethal tusks, so it too must be exceptionally tasty.

One of the best examples of the tiger's exceptional design is his teeth. He has four canines, each about three inches long, the lower closing into a groove in the upper pair. These canines are flattened laterally, the upper ones pointed with a sharp cutting edge behind. The cubs' milk teeth are gradually replaced by the adult set. The canines grow alongside the milk teeth so that the cub has some double teeth before the milk teeth drop out. The fourteen molars are strong and can easily crush bones; it is these teeth that chew the food into pieces small enough to swallow. The twelve small incisors gnaw the flesh off the bone of the prey before the tongue rasps it clean.

> In what distant deeps or skies
> Burned the fire of thine eyes?[2]

In these lines from 'The Tiger', William Blake refers to the characteristic glare of the tiger's eye. The tiger has phenomenal eyesight. Unlike most animals he has in-depth vision, but unless the subject actually moves, however slightly, he cannot distinguish it. Most cats can see in the dark, a necessary trait for those who hunt at night, and possess an efficient optical system whereby the reflecting layers behind the retina are highly developed, throwing back even the dullest rays of light through the pupils. These rays contract the receptor cells both on the way in and on the way out, stimulating them each time. Their reflection lights up the eyes in the beam of a lamp producing 'the electric glare of feline eyes'.[3] The ancient Chinese believed that tigers actually generated light in their eyes, rather like a car's headlights, so that they could see in the dark.

The yellowish-brown quartz that is sometimes used in jewellery known as 'tiger's eye' is a fairly good representation of the real thing during the day. At night tigers' eyes are pale emerald to blue when they reflect moon-light, but appear bright red when caught in the beam of a torch.

Trackers in Indonesia would cut the hairs in their noses in the belief that tigers could hear the sound of the air passing through these hairs. How necessary a precaution that was is debatable, but many hunters have been convinced that the tiger could hear them breathe as they sat in a *machán*, or platform hide, in a tree. A tiger must have exceptional hearing or else he would not be able to hunt on a dark night with neither moon nor stars to see by. Sometimes the elephant grass and bamboo thickets he inhabits are extremely dense so he must rely on his hypersensitive hearing in order to locate his prey.

The ears themselves are small with a white spot on the back of each. There seems no logical explanation for this mark, although it has been suggested that the spots are a warning sign of aggression when swivelled forward; however, when the tiger is really angry he will lay his ears flat, so masking the spots. These spots on the tigress's ears help the cubs to follow her when she is leading them through thick bush.

Perhaps the least developed of all the tiger's senses is smell. Undoubtedly tigers do have olfactory organs but these seem to be markedly less effective than his other senses. However, the tiger is quick to pick up the scent of other tigers left as marks or of tigresses on heat that are not calling, even though he does not rely on scent to hunt, for he will continue to stalk live prey while passing over an edible carcass that is out of sight.

Apart from acute sight and hearing, the tiger has another aid for locating prey: experience. He knows his own home range intimately and is aware of all the likely places where food can be found, the waterholes, day shelters and open grazing land. He can also recognize certain signs which suggest that food may be lurking nearby such as the presence of monkeys in the trees. Monkeys are generally messy eaters who throw aside half-eaten fruits. These attract the little chital deer, who could not normally reach the fruit high up in the trees. The chital also know that the monkeys, from their high vantage point, can see and warn them of any approaching danger. The tiger on the other hand knows equally well the likelihood of finding chital deer below or nearby these chattering monkeys.

Although the chital hind makes a single good meal for the tiger, the heavier stag at around 200 pounds will last for at least two days. Often described as the most beautiful deer in the world, they make easy prey for the tiger although their numbers are now much depleted.

The larger the deer the fewer the number of kills the tiger needs to make to satisfy his hunger. Sometimes he has to make do with the little hog deer, the swamp or barking deer, even perhaps a blue nilgai or an Indian antelope if more substantial fare is not available.

Farmers for centuries have been quick to condemn the tiger as an inveterate cattle-lifter, but this is an unfair accusation as the tiger infinitely prefers wild animals to domestic stock. By choice the tiger would only go for wild pig and large deer, animals that were once common throughout the whole of his original range.

Wild boars are black, brown or grey in colour with a full mane of black bristles. They can weigh up to 500 pounds. With this enormous bulk, long razor sharp tusks and an unlikely agility they make a formidable opponent. Sambar deer are also common tiger prey. They are the largest of the Asian deer, some stags reaching almost

700 pounds. They keep the same hours and occupy the same habitat as the tiger which makes them exceptionally wary creatures. They have a loud barking alarm note and, like most other deer, stamp the ground as a danger signal. They also *pook* or *bell* which, when repeated, is a sure sign of the presence of a tiger. This *pooking* sound is also made by the tiger which is strange, for as a danger signal it can hardly attract a sambar to its foe.

It needs a strong, intelligent tiger to tackle a gaur for these animals are massive, sometimes weighing as much as a ton and always exceptionally alert. The bulls are dark brown to black with heavy horns, while the females and young bull calves are a light dun colour. They inhabit the dark interiors of the dense forest through which they move with great ease on surprisingly small white feet. Gaur calves are the most likely prey for tigers as the adults are fierce and often retaliate, sometimes with the whole herd ringing the tiger to protect a victim.

Wild buffalo also provide a handsome meal. They, like the gaur, are wary animals and, despite their bulk are fleet of foot, speeding through the forest at the first scent of danger. Young rhinoceroses and elephants can also fall foul of the tiger but the actual numbers killed are infinitesimal compared with other prey species.

Although a carnivore, a tiger will eat a variety of food if driven by shortage of natural prey species. Like the domestic cat tigers eat grass, presumably for the same reason, to cleanse their stomachs. Grasshoppers and locusts are other delicacies for the tiger as are land crabs and occasionally crocodile eggs. There is a Chinese story of a man carrying a sack of croaking frogs who was killed by a tiger: the man's body was abandoned untouched but the sack was ripped open and the frogs devoured.

Even fish are sometimes caught by tigers. When the streams dry up leaving pools, the fish are stranded and a tiger can whisk them out with his paw. Surely apocryphal is the Malay tale of the tiger who, feeling like a little fishing, crept up to the river bank and sat with his tail in the water. As soon as he got a bite he flipped it swiftly out of the water and the fish landed on the ground in front of him.

Another doubtful, but amusing, story is an Indian account of how a tiger catches monkeys:

The monkeys, at his first approach, give warning by their confused chattering, and immediately take themselves to the highest and smallest twigs of the trees; when the tiger, seeing them out of his reach, and sensible of their fright, lies couchant under the tree and then falls aroaring; at which they, trembling, let go their hold, and tumbling down, he picks them up to satisfy his hunger.[4]

Choice, chance, curiosity, weakness or hunger will cause a tiger to vary his appetite. Much has been written on this point, real and apocryphal, but more nonsense has been written on his supposed lust for man than on any other aspect of the tiger. A man-eating tiger can be defined as one that deliberately kills humans for food and he is extremely rare. Tigers do kill humans for many reasons, to protect their cubs, out of fear, from surprise, when wounded or if interrupted during courtship, but these killers cannot be classed as man-eaters. The number of true man-eaters has always been a tiny percentage of the whole tiger population yet, because their story always sounds more dramatic, the whole species for centuries has carried this mark of Cain. Hunters have perpetrated this reputation because it makes them out to be braver and more noble. To avenge a poor villager who has lost a child, to rid the countryside of an especially dangerous animal or to slay a proven man-eater seems infinitely more glorious than to merely shoot at a driven beast. The tiger has been further vilified because frequently any unexplained missing person or murdered corpse has been attributed to the presence of a man-eater prowling the neighbourhood.

Jim Corbett, a relentless slayer of man-eaters and author of dozens of essays on the subject, maintained that the tiger was always driven to man-eating by circumstances beyond his control and had never begun life with a lust for human flesh. In most cases he found upon examination that the man-eater he had killed had already been wounded, either by man or by a difficult prey like a porcupine or large wild boar. Unable to stalk his usual prey with success, the tiger had turned to the easiest available form of meat, *man*. Other man-eaters Corbett investigated had worn-out claws or broken canines or both. Too old or inactive to stalk with skill, they had resorted to lying in wait for unsuspecting villagers. He felt that occasionally a tiger would attack humans when other wild animals were scarce and they were genuinely short of food, as in the barren heights of Kumaon.

Corbett cites many examples of tigers adopting the unnatural diet of human flesh. One young tigress had lost an eye and had been pierced by over fifty quills after an encounter with a porcupine. She had tried to remove the quills with her teeth but without success, so she had had to remain where she was in the long grass, licking her wounds and starving for lack of food. A woman cutting grass for her cattle had backed into the tigress who struck a fatal blow to the woman's head but left her untouched. The animal limped about a mile away and sheltered in a hollow under a fallen tree. Later a man came to cut firewood and the tigress, lying on the far side, grabbed his naked chest and killed him. Perhaps the blood gave her the idea that this was a way to satisfy her acute hunger as he was eventually found with part of his back eaten. The next day she killed her third victim, without provocation, and became a confirmed man-eater. She was finally slain after her tally had reached twenty-four.

Had the tigress had cubs, she could well have taught them to hunt humans. However, when they left her to live independently they would probably have abandoned the habit.

A human makes a scant meal for the tiger and is likely to be unpalatable as well. In order to survive the man-eater would have to kill other prey animals. A question that has yet to be answered is why would a man-eater bother with man in the first place if he were agile enough to tackle normal prey animals?

One of the most notorious regions in the past for man-eaters was the Sundarbans, that vast delta of the Ganges, particularly when the river was in flood and game was scarce. Captain Williamson commented in 1807:

> Royal Tigers are often seen swimming across the various rivers which form the innumerable islands inhabited only by wild beasts and presenting an immense barrier all along the sea coast from Saugor Island to the great mouth of the Megna.[5]

These tigers were the scourge of the salt-panners' life for as soon as one was sighted the panners would

> take to flight, and conceal themselves in caves excavated for the purpose; from which, it however sometimes happens, the hungry animal removes every obstacle with his claws, and drags out one or more of the inhabitants, already half dead with terror.[6]

One of the earliest writers on the man-eaters of the Sundarbans, he remarked:

> it is very well known that if ten men are in company, they will single out one particular person from the rest; and they also seldom care to attack a white man, if a black man be among them (plate 46). The reason for the making of this distinction is, probably, that they are better aquainted with the black men, and had rather prey upon them, than upon Europeans, to whom they are strangers.[7]

The tiger's hold over man's imagination does not result merely from a fear of the tiger as a man-eater. The beauty of the creature's form, the economy of his movements and the contained strength of his body have all combined to make the tiger a potent symbol for many of man's highest aspirations.

5

Under a pipal tree
Lockwood Kipling

The tiger is the spirit of the jungle. Even his distant roar, or an alarm call from some startled animal announcing his arrival, changes the atmosphere. Man, too, has been greatly moved by his powerful presence and has inevitably been affected by the tension he creates. Not surprisingly, legends, beliefs, and folk tales have grown up around the tiger, just as he has been portrayed in the art and literature of all those who have lived near enough to hear him, to see his victims, or to have been his prey.

Perhaps the man-eating tiger has fuelled the most creative fantasies. For just as some people believed they obtained special powers from eating certain animals, so they also feared that the tiger might gain some of man's more magical properties from eating human flesh. The man-eater thus became closely associated with the human spirit, especially the spirit of his victim. A typical example of this belief from central India shows how the spirit of a man-eater's victim tried to protect his killer.

A native hunter, keen to revenge a victim, sat up in a tree over the corpse. The man-eater approached to finish his feast when the corpse raised a warning arm pointing to the hunter in the tree. The tiger retreated and the hunter pegged the offending hand to the ground with a bamboo, then climbed into another tree. The tiger returned but again was warned off by the other hand, and so fled. The hunter pegged this hand in a like manner and resumed his vigil. When the tiger returned there was no free hand for the spirit to warn its new charge and the hunter took his revenge.

In many of the Asian folk-tales certain men can change at will into a tiger. Lockwood Kipling, Rudyard's father, cites one Bengali legend of a man 'who by traffic with demons had acquired a charm which enabled him to change into a tiger'. His wife, 'being as curious as the rest of the daughters of Eve, begged to be allowed to watch the transformation. Reluctantly he consented and entrusted her with a magic root to be given to him to restore him to his natural state. When the tiger appeared before her she panicked and ran away in terror. Before she could recover the villagers chased her away. She never saw her husband again, and died broken hearted. He revenged himself by attacking and killing the villagers.' Kipling adds that 'such a tale should be told under a pipal tree, whispering of ghost-land overhead. Under such circumstances animal transformations assume a dignity and credibility.'[1]

If a man could change into a tiger, then the reverse might be possible. Such a creature, a tiger in human form, was called a *tuindak*. *Tuindaks* were supposed to be quite common in the more primitive Indian and Malay villages which was why the inhabitants would never dare say the word 'tiger' or reveal where one could be found in case they were talking to a *tuindak*. Belief in the *tuindak* could be used to advantage as in this Malay legend of a husband disposing of his unfaithful wife's hermit lover:

One evening a wife went to fetch water from a well near a village. A tiger sprang and attempted to carry her off. Her husband rushed to the rescue and speared the tiger through the stomach. The tiger escaped, severely wounded, with the spear still in his belly. The trail of blood was followed to the hut of a hermit who lived at the edge of the forest. The blood led up the ladder and into the hut. The villagers called out to the hermit, but there was no reply. Wary, thinking the tiger had taken the man as well, they entered the hut to find the owner dead on the floor. The same spear that the husband had injured the tiger with was firmly imbedded in the stomach of the man.

Many of the European hunters experienced a certain reluctance in their normally brave *shikaris*, native hunting guides, to pursue a man-eater. They attributed this reluctance to a fear of a 'malign power which no rifle could combat'. If natives were forced to follow up such a tiger they would do so in a 'frenzied crowd and to the accompaniment of drums and fireworks'.[2]

In many cases where a man-eater preyed on a particular village it was this fear of witchcraft rather than a lack of courage that prevented the village hunter from killing the tiger. Apart from man-eating there were other ways of recognizing a weretiger or *tuindak*. Just as the devil is portrayed with cloven hoofs in European mythology so the weretiger leaves a trail of human hand- or foot-prints in the earth. Since the pug marks of a lame tiger can look like human foot-prints and being lame can also turn him into a man-eater it is easy to see how this legend developed.

Tuindaks were both feared and revered. Overawed by their strange magical qualities, the natives often treated them as minor deities. They believed that their powers could be harnessed both ways: a goat, chicken or buffalo sacrificed to a tiger deity might act as a palliative and ward off danger, equally such a sacrificial gift might obtain his assistance. If a new, troublesome tiger made an appearance in the vicinity, then an offering might engage his support against a newcomer.

These beliefs in the magical properties of man-eaters and weretigers encouraged the actual worship of tigers themselves, quite common in India in a variety of forms. Forest tribes deep in tiger country were obviously the most impressionable and nowhere is this more evident than in Bengal around the notorious Sundarbans. There the presiding deity of tigers is called Daksin Ray. It is thought that Daksin Ray was a skilful hunter in the Sundarbans, killing many tigers and revenging many deaths. By degrees he became deified into an important tiger god. Similarly, in the middle of the last century a Captain Pole shot a prodigious number of tigers in Travancore in the Deccan. When he died the natives laid offerings on his grave in order to 'propitiate his spirit and invoke his continued aid against wild beasts'.[3]

Daksin Ray is still worshipped in temples built in his honour by all who come into contact with tigers, especially wood-cutters, graziers and boatmen. These temples range from an elaborate stone edifice to a simple mound of earth or a flat stone, sometimes even an old banyan tree; in the Sundarbans practically every tree is a shrine to him. He is always represented with divine features, carrying bow and arrow and often astride a tiger.

Bengali folk literature is full of tiger stories. Daksin Ray had a foolproof method of ensuring that he was adequately glorified by poets and writers. The tiger god told the poets that if they found anyone who did not approve of what they had written about Daksin Ray then the offenders and their families would be 'extirpated with the help of the tigers'![4]

Daksin Ray was a powerful god and those who invoked his help with enough prayer and offerings were well rewarded. In one Bengali story a loyal son, Puspadetta, went in search of his father. When he was taken prisoner by King Surath he sang the praises of Daksin

Ray. The next day, as he was about to be executed, a troop of tigers entered the city of Turgana and began to kill the inhabitants and the king's soldiers. The tigers also tore off the whiskers and the beard of the chief of police who later died. The god himself arrived in a chariot and slew the king. But the story has a happy ending: the son found his father, and King Surath's wife implored Daksin Ray to restore her husband to her, to which he consented.

In other parts of India tiger cults took different forms. The Bhils of Rajputana, for instance, fervently believed that they were all descended from tigers. In Nepal, magnificent festivals are still held in which the villagers don tiger masks and dance in the tiger's honour.

In China, from the very earliest times, the tiger has been associated with the most basic tenets. Star and animal worship, branches of Animism or Universism, was common to all nomadic tribes, shepherds and hunters living in the open. In *I Ching, The Book of Changes,* the white tiger, *Pai Hu*, represents autumn. To the Chinese this analogy was appropriate as the tiger, like the stormy season, was particularly ferocious at that time of year, noisily on the rampage, roaring for a mate and terrorizing humans. *Pai Hu* also represented the west. The Chinese believed that this great white tiger was the reincarnation of the star, Alpha, or the whole constellation of Ursa Major. This tiger star lives in the 'silver stream of heaven', known in the West as the Milky Way.

For the mortal tiger, *Hu*, to attain the Milky Way he must first live for 500 years, whereupon he becomes *Pai Hu*. The mark of *wang* 王, or king, is formed on his forehead. The fact that most tigers bear some form of this mark at birth does not seem to upset the story (plate 32). The tiger became immortal after one thousand years and then, as chief of all the quadrupeds, could inhabit the 'silver stream of heaven' or the moon in whatever form he chose in his new title of *Pai chon chih ch'ang*.

According to *I Ching* two energizing and regulating forces, the *Tao*, come from the universe. These forces are known as *yin* and *yang* and in the natural science aspect of Taoism, *Fêng Shui*, they are often represented as the tiger and the dragon, as well as wind and water. The basis of Taoism is that everything in heaven and earth, animate and inanimate, has a soul. The soul is either good, controlled by *yang*, the green dragon, or evil, controlled by *yin*, the white tiger. These animal deities are all-important as they control the grave sites of the Taoist's ancestors who in turn protect the living. If the dragon force is dominant then the ancestors are appeased and no harm can come to the living; but if the white tiger controls the grave, then disaster is assured for the descendants.

Yin and *yang* are normally in opposition but occasionally they work against each other for eventual good. According to *I Ching, The Book of Changes* 'the breath of the tiger creates the wind and the breath of the dragon creates the clouds; together they create the rain which fructifies the earth and brings forth food for mankind.'[5] In a drought real tiger bones would be dropped down a 'dragon' well which would so enrage the presiding dragon that the fracas would cause a storm ending in torrential rain.

Mythical or real, the Chinese have always feared the tiger, for they believe this ferocious animal destroys others by absorbing their evil qualities. When a man became insane or delirious he was described as having a tiger obsession, the complaint being known as 'transference into a tiger'.

The role of the tiger as a symbol of *yin*, or evil, was reversed with the advent of Buddhism when the animal was regarded as an exemplary character with the qualities of *yang*. Purged of his vicious and rapacious nature, the nobility of the tiger's form, the beauty of his colour, his proportion and grace of movement, coupled with his strength and ferocity, have made the tiger the apt symbol of the power, grandeur and glory of the Buddhist faith. Here he has obtained immortality. Deified and worshipped, he is a prevalent symbol and a favourite subject in Buddhist paintings – usually combined with his old adversary the dragon, against a background of bamboo and possibly a waterfall as well.

Symbolism and nature are inextricably linked in Buddhist paintings, like the tiger and bamboo (plate 22). Since the bamboo bends in the wind its presence with the tiger is thought to show the hospitality of the weak for the strong. Another interpretation is that only the tiger can enter a bamboo thicket. A bamboo lashed by wind and rain suggests a wild jungle, symbolizing sin, which the tiger, representing the human spirit, has to find a way through. Both the tiger and the waterfall are considered fast and furious.

The earliest Buddhist pictures of tigers in China date from the eighth century and in Japan from a little later; they are still popular today. As there were no tigers in Japan, their artists had to rely on Chinese works to copy. The Japanese portrayed the tiger as a spiritual idea and not as a natural history study. One Japanese artist answered a Western critic who said that his tiger was incorrect anatomically with: 'Yes possibly, but it is morally perfect.'

Although the Japanese artist Ganku (1749-1838) had ample opportunity to study tigers at first hand on his patron's estate, he still preferred to portray them in the traditional Japanese style. One famous tiger of his is, in fact, a tiger skin without bones, painted in exceptional detail with an impressionistic back-ground. The real tigers, imported from Korea by his patron, Mayedo, remain unrecorded.

The Japanese also 'borrowed' the myths and folk legends that had evolved around the tiger in China. The major ascetics either rode tigers or kept them as their constant companions. One of the best known stories, *Toro no ko Watashi*, *The Wise Mother*, illustrates the sagacity of the tigress (plate 23):

> A tigress had three cubs, one of which was vicious and could not, with safety, be left with the other two. The mother was obliged to take them across the river, but could only carry one at a time. She devised a plan by which she made seven different journeys across the water, carrying the ill-tempered one back and forth while she left the others on the opposite banks.[6]

This is the Far Eastern version of the European riddle of the farmer who wanted to cross a river with a fox, a goose and a sack of corn.

Another folk-tale of the tiger, this time duped by a fox, is called 'The Fox that Borrowed the Dignity of the Tiger':

> One day a fox was ambushed and caught by a tiger. It was too late to flee and in strength the fox was no match for the striped one. Therefore the fox said, 'You think you are the strongest animal on earth, don't you? Wait a moment before you devour me; haven't you heard that this is no longer the case and that nowadays I am the most powerful?' 'No', answered the tiger, 'such nonsense!' 'Come along then,' said the fox 'and I'll show you.' Thereupon they went for a walk in the forest, the fox in front, the tiger behind him. All the animals ran off helter-skelter as soon as they saw these two. 'There you are,' said the fox, 'now you have seen for yourself how much they fear me.' Completely convinced by this clinching argument, the tiger retired with caution to a safe distance and then ran off like the wind.[7]

Perhaps a variation of this tale was the basis of Aesop's fable of 'The Tiger and the Fox' (plate 24):

> A skilful archer coming into the woods directed his arrows so successfully that he slew many wild beasts, and wounded many others. This put the whole savage kind into a great consternation, and made them fly into the most retired thickets for refuge. At last the tiger resumed courage and bidding them not to be afraid, said

17   Scroll painting of a Muslim riding a spotted tiger god from Santal Parganas, Bengal, circa 1930

18   Bronze belt-hook in
the form of a leaping tiger
from the Ordos region, central China,
circa A.D. 100-200

19   This chape (the metal tip to a
scabbard) is from Uzbekistan, central
Asia, circa 1,000-800 B.C. It is made
of bronze inlaid with silver and shows
a tiger attacking a goat while itself
being attacked by some strange beast

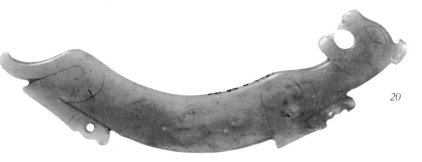

20   Green jade amulet given to
Chinese troops in the Han
dynasty, circa A.D. 100-200

21   A fine example of an early marble
Chinese tiger of the Shang
dynasty, 1,300-1,100 B.C.

22   A Chinese hanging scroll in ink on paper entitled 'A Tiger by a Stream with Bamboo and Waterfall' by Mu Ch'i, thirteenth century

23   Chinese hanging scroll entitled 'A Tigress and Three Cubs' after Chao Yuan, fourteenth century.

24   Engraving illustrating Aesop's fable 'The Tiger and the Fox'

he alone would engage the enemy, telling them that they might depend on his valour to avenge their wrongs. In the midst of these threats, while he was lashing himself with his tail, and tearing at the ground with anger, an arrow pierced his ribs, and hung by its barbed point in his side. He set up a loud and hideous roar occasioned by the anguish he felt, and endeavoured to draw out the painful dart with his teeth; when the fox approaching him inquired with an air of surprise who it was that could have strength and courage enough to wound so mighty and valourous a beast? 'Ah', said the tiger, 'I was mistaken in my reckoning — it was that invincible man younder.'[8]

Two stories with one application: brains always triumph over strength.

6

There is a raging tiger inside every man
Murray Kempton

No single animal has influenced art, literature, legend, religious cults, attitudes and ideas more than the tiger. His image of power and malevolence, magnificence and nobility, is second to none. His presence has always fascinated man; some have sought to imprison him in a cage while others have wished to extinguish him by killing. But before the advent of Western man with his gun, the tiger had few natural enemies and was free to roam in huge numbers from the Hindu Kush to Siberia, from the Mediterranean Sea to the Pacific Ocean. In those days, with optimum conditions, death from illness was rare, the tiger being a relatively disease-free animal, and other predators were rightly wary of 'the monarch of the jungle'.

On very rare occasions a tiger may be attacked by wild dogs hunting in a pack. About the size of red setters, the wild dogs' usual prey is wild pig or deer but they have been known to tackle a tiger, an act prompted not by hunger but by sheer devilment. There are many accounts of such conflicts although no one has recorded witnessing an actual death. Partially eaten tigers have been found surrounded by savaged dogs amid signs of a considerable fight. Usually the tiger is not accustomed to being attacked so has no defensive mechanism. Surrounded by wild dogs the tiger becomes confused, indignant and powerless to do more than snarl, swipe and claw, which may not be enough against a large number of attackers.

Crocodiles will go for a tiger's kill and so fall foul of the owner. They have been known to take tiger cubs while they are drinking at the water's edge but accounts of a crocodile attacking a full-grown tiger and dragging it under water to drown sound far-fetched.

Before the arrival of Europeans in India and south-east Asia with their superior firearms, man and the tiger lived in comparative harmony. A proven man-eating tiger might be killed to protect a village or he might be slain for his magnificent pelt. Occasionally the ruling classes might kill for sport but such primitive methods were used for killing or ensnaring that the numbers actually destroyed were never excessive; the tiger as a species was never really threatened.

One of the most common methods employed was to drive the tiger forward into nets. The tiger, fleeing from a noisy crowd throwing fire-crackers and beating gongs, would rush headlong into a strong net which would collapse about him, entangling his vicious claws, so that he could be killed with spears and clubs, sometimes days later, by even the most cowardly. Strong bamboo cages baited with goats were another way of capturing a tiger safely. Another popular method was to aim an elaborate crossbow, which fired a poisoned arrow, on a known tiger trail and rig it with a system of trip wires. Hopefully, the tiger would set off the trip wire and the arrow would pierce his skin. When the wound was licked clean, the poison would cause his tongue to swell and so the tiger would suffocate.

The Manchu Tartars preferred to trap their tigers. They would dig a wide circular ditch which they covered with brushwood. An 'island' was left in the middle where a man sat as human bait. It was hoped that the tiger, seeing the man, would spring, land on the flimsy brushwood and fall into the ditch. The human bait hoped that his colleagues had dug the ditch wide enough. Once caught in the ditch the tiger could be easily speared.

Other forms of pits and traps have been, and regretfully still are, used to good effect to kill tigers. These range from the hand-dug holes with sharpened bamboo spikes to the modern gin trap with its wicked steel claws. Such methods are hardly honourable in killing an animal but, recorded in the memoirs of the Mogul Emperor Akbar Khan (1566-1605) is an account of how bird lime, a mixture of mustard oil and latex from the *pipal* tree, used to be smeared on leaves and hay around a bait. When the tiger approached his paws became covered with the mixture. The more he tried to clean his claws the more clogged they became, his tongue swelled up and, frantic from asphyxiation, he rolled helplessly onto his back. Thus incapacitated he was easily killed with spears.

Since man first began to hunt, the tiger has been speared, trapped and later poisoned but always in moderation (plate 39). From the earliest civilizations tigers have been kept in captivity, especially in those countries where they were not indigenous. There were no wild tigers in Europe, the nearest in classical times were in eastern Turkey, or according to Pliny the Elder, at Hyrcania, Iran and Iraq, all countries under the sway of the Medes and Persians until the advent of Alexander the Great. He marched his army across great tracts of country inhabited by tigers and complained bitterly that they attacked his baggage trains as he moved eastwards towards the Indus. It is not surprising to find that the earliest-known tigers in captivity in the West were those presented to the citizens of Athens by King Seleucus I Nicator (315-312 BC), a former general under Alexander. Τιγρις in classical Greek means arrow and, just as they had named the fastest-flowing river in their Empire *Tigris*, so they called their swiftest animal by the same name.

The Romans, too, kept tigers in captivity for the elder Pliny records in his *Naturalis Historiæ* that Augustus Octavianus – Julius Caesar's great-nephew and adopted son – was given 'an unspecified number of tigers'. Pliny continues 'Augustus also, in the consulship of Marcus Tibero and Paullus Fabius, at the dedication of the theatre of Marcellus on 7 May was the first of all persons at Rome who exhibited a tame tiger in a cage, although his late majesty Claudius exhibited four at one time.'[1] Pliny seems to have his dates confused as the dedication was 11 BC and Claudius ruled from 41-54 AD. Seneca recorded an account of a tigress who was kissed by its keeper in the arena in the reign of Nero.

On the whole, tigers were to be admired and not wasted in the arena in fights; that was left to the ubiquitous lion. The fact that tigers were rare and difficult to capture may have given them an exalted status. Pliny the elder gives advice on how to catch a tiger cub in safety in Book VIII of *Naturalis Historiæ*:

> This is a description of how a huntsman, having seized some [tiger] cubs, would gallop off with them on the swiftest and freshest horse. When the outraged tigress discovered her loss she would rush headlong into pursuit and at her furious approach he would drop one of the cubs in the hope of delaying her onrush. But she would pick it up and as though spurred on by its weight continue the chase coming closer and closer to her enemy until he was safely on shipboard and she was left to vent her fury on shore.[2]

John Guillim, in *Display of Heraldrie*, 1724, describes another method:

> Some report that those who rob the tiger of her young, use a policy to detain their dam from following them, by casting sundry looking glasses in the way, whereat she useth long to gaze,

whether it be to behold her own beauty, or because, when she seeth her shape in the glass, she thinketh she sees one of her young ones, and so they escape the swiftness of her pursuit. And thus are many deceived of the substance, whilst they are much busied about the shadows.[3]

Fig. 5   Arms of the de Bardis family showing heraldic tiger and looking-glass

In England the first recorded tiger kept in captivity belonged to King Henry I who established a menagerie at Woodstock, near Oxford, as early as 1120. The menagerie flourished in the reign of King Henry III with gifts from foreign potentates. One such gift, a tiger, came from Frederick II, that highly intelligent Holy Roman Emperor also known as 'Stupor Mundi', in 1250. Two years later King Henry III had the whole zoo transferred to the Tower of London where it remained for several hundred years, rousing the fury of the sheriffs of London who complained bitterly at being ordered to pay fourpence a day for the upkeep of the animals.

The Tower Menagerie flourished or not according to the monarch's interest in animals and the numbers of gifts of exotica received from foreign rulers. Tigers do not seem to be mentioned anywhere in Tudor times so presumably they were not to be seen in England. Thus it is not surprising that English artists, sculptors and wood-carvers portrayed the tiger so inaccurately and crudely for they would have relied on descriptions in classical writings.

Presumably, one of the Stuart Kings received a diplomatic gift of a tiger, for the playwright John Evelyn described its condition in the Tower Menagerie as pitiful in 1644, adding that in Florence that City's 'wolves, cats, bears, tigers and lions' were kept in a deep walled court, and were 'therefore to be seen with much more pleasure than those at the Tower of London in their grates'.[4] The public were not admitted to the Tower Menagerie until the middle of the eighteenth century and then only on the payment of three half-pennies or the gift of a dead dog or a cat. However, the public had a chance to see tigers in the travelling menageries that were not uncommon from the turn of the eighteenth century onwards, as one Hannah Twynny found to her cost. Her epitaph in Malmesbury Abbey reads:

> In bloom of life
> She's snatched from hence,
> She had not room
> To make defence:
> For tyger fierce
> Took life away
> And here she lies
> In a bed of clay
> Until the Resurrection Day.

Apparently this Hannah Twynny, a servant-girl from the White Lion Inn, was attacked and killed by a tiger that escaped from a travelling menagerie as early as 1704.

To possess a wild beast in captivity gave glory to the owner; it also gave him a sense of power over nature and he hoped to gain some measure of reflected strength from being able to curtail the freedom of such a noble animal.

Hunters, too, believed that a tiger killed in equal combat brought greatness upon the hunter. Just as the man who killed a deer tended to believe he was swifter and more alert than his quarry, so the tiger-slayer felt that he had shown he was more courageous than the tiger. For, up to the middle of the eighteenth century, however much of a local nuisance a tiger might be and however much man might enjoy killing or capturing him, he was still considered a magnificent quarry. He was highly esteemed for his strength, his speed, his prodigious power and his ferocity. He might be a problem to the occasional village and he might be feared as a man-eater in the Sundarbans but he had not yet become a menace to man. As land in Asia was still plentiful, the growing population could expand without impinging on virgin forest or jungle, and agriculturalists and foresters could increase cultivation without incursion into tiger territory.

But towards the end of the eighteenth century, the situation in Asia slowly began to change. The population expanded and Europeans began to arrive in increasing numbers. They brought with them new attitudes towards agriculture and industry as well as roads and railways and a new way of regarding man's relationship with his environment and with animals. Man was supreme and any animal which obstructed him ought to be destroyed. Europeans also brought superior firearms.

In India the British were soon firmly established. They had come to trade but had stayed to conquer and, as conquerors, they were the master race. Others tilled and toiled, so they had little to occupy them and many spent a great deal of time playing polo, pig-sticking, hunting, shooting, fishing and killing (plate 25).

Until then the number of tigers slain had been quickly replaced by natural means which had made their numbers seemingly inexhaustible. But now they were branded as the 'scourge of humanity', they were seen as 'the obstacle to the advance of population and tillage'[5] and the destruction of the tiger on a large scale became a humanitarian task which gave the doer a good Christian conscience. 'It was much that I had been the avenger, constituted by Him, who ordains all things, to slay these tigers, and to save further loss of life.'[6] The mass extermination of tigers had the added advantage of being 'the most exciting and glorious sport this world affords' and 'one worthy of gentlemen'.[7]

One native ruler of a province to the south of India deserves mention. He epitomized the old ways and the old cult of the tiger but became embroiled in war with the advancing British, which caused his own death and the downfall of his state. His name was Tipu Sultan. His father, Haidar Ali, had taken command of the Province of Mysore in the middle of the eighteenth century. Just before his son was born, Haidar Ali had consulted a holy man called Tipu Sultan, Tipu meaning tiger or conqueror of the woods, and Sultan the royal title meaning conqueror of the passions. Out of a deep respect for this holy man, the heir apparent was named after him and later he became known by his people and the British as the Tiger of Mysore.

Tipu Sultan believed that it was better to live two days as a tiger than two hundred as a sheep. Tigers were his life. He had a tiger throne, and tiger stripes adorned all his possessions, his clothes and the uniforms of his soldiers. Even his handkerchiefs bore the tiger stripe, a *bubberee*, which 'no person presumed to adopt but by particular order'. His weapons, so superbly fashioned at the Royal Arsenal at Seringapatam, were richly adorned with tigers: stripes were incorporated into the rifle barrels while their stocks (plate 44), hammers (plate 45), engravings and even the tiny sights all bore

25   'Tom Raw in Danger, Tiger Hunting with Elephants'. Tom Raw, the Griffin, was a new boy in the East India Company whose antics were depicted in a series of prints by Sir Charles D'Oyly published in 1828

26   Gold and enamel pocket watch made for the Chinese market in the early nineteenth century

27   'Tipu's Tiger', Seringapatam, Mysore, India. This model of a British East India Company officer lying recumbent and being mauled by a tiger was made for the amusement of Tipu Sultan, ruler of Mysore, in about 1790 and was found in the palace after the storming of Seringapatam by troops under General Harris in 1799. Inside the model is a miniature organ with a keyboard and bellows designed to simulate the groans of the dying man and the roars of delight of the tiger. The painted wood model is Indian but the mechanics are French

28   South Staffordshire painted enamel on copper snuffbox in the form of a tiger, circa 1770

29   The Eighteenth (Royal Irish) Regiment of Foot at the storming of the fortress of Amoy, 26 August 1841 which was defended by the terrifying tiger-men

31   A charging tiger in the Royal Chitawan National Park

32   The mark of *Wang*, 王, on the forehead of a tiger in the Royal Chitawan National Park

33   A tigress resting in the heat of the day in Kanha National Park, India

34   A tiger fishing?

35   A white tiger of Rewa. This is not an albino but a 'recessive mutant' with brownish-grey stripes on a white background and bluish eyes

36   Tiger courtship is a noisy and often violent affair where mating takes place a prodigious number of times over a period of several days

37   The tigress is a devoted mother and will move her cubs at the slightest sign of danger by carrying them by the head between her canine teeth

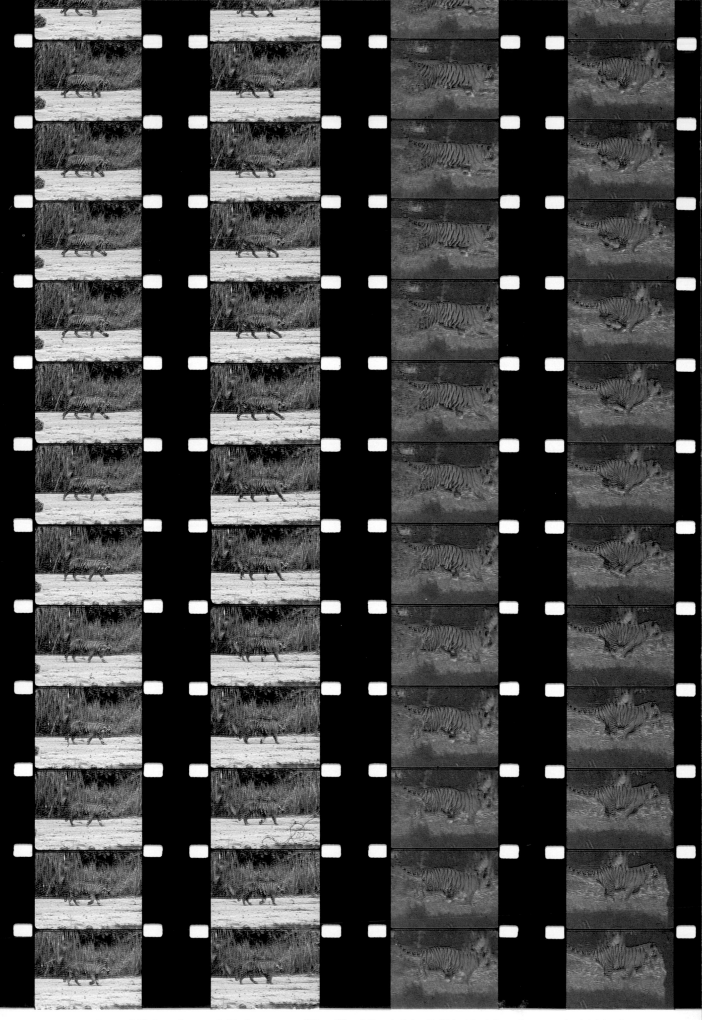

38   Stills from the remarkable documentary 'Tiger, Tiger' (Survival Anglia Television) show the unusual gait of the tiger

decorations of parts of the tiger. His banner carried the words 'The Tiger is God' in Canarese and, when doubled up, it resembled the face of a tiger (plate 42).

The Tiger of Mysore ruled savagely from a tiger throne:

> of considerable beauty and magnificence (plate 40). The support was a wooden tiger as large as life, covered with gold, in the attitude of standing, his head and forelegs appeared in the front, and under the throne, which was placed across his back. It was composed of an octagonal frame, eight feet by five, surrounded by a low railing, on which were ten small tiger heads, made of gold, and beautifully inlaid with precious stones; the ascent to the throne was by small silver steps on each side. From the centre of the back part, opposite the large tiger's head (plate 47), a gilded iron pillar rose, seven feet high, surmounted by a canopy superbly decorated with a fringe of pearls (plate 40). The whole was made of wood and covered with a thin sheet of the purest gold, richly illuminated with tiger stripes, and Arabic verses.[8]

Tipu Sultan was a fanatical Muslim, with an obsessive loathing of the infidel, particularly the British who had whittled away his father's and his own territory. He had fought at the Battle of Porto Novo in 1781 in the second Mysore War when Sir Hector Munro had humbled him and his father. From that day on his desire to belittle the white man increased and became entangled with his tiger obsession. British prisoners were kept in filth and hunger until strangled, impaled and then thrown to tigers. Even

> the walls of the houses in the main streets of Seringapatam had been ornamented by the Sultan's command, with full length caricatures of the English. In one it was a tiger seizing a trembling Englishman, in another it was a horseman cutting off two heads at a blow, ... but the more favourite caricatures are necessarily excluded from the decorative narrative.[9]

Another account mentions:

> a row of white faced Feringhees (Europeans) their hands tied behind them, and their faces half blackened. There were some being torn to pieces by tigers while men of the faith looked on and applauded.[10]

Today Tipu Sultan is probably best remembered for 'Tipu's Tiger', the famous man-tiger organ that has delighted thousands of visitors to the Victoria and Albert Museum in London (plate 27). It seems likely that Tipu Sultan had the idea for commissioning such a macabre piece, a mechanical tiger savaging a European, on hearing how his old adversary, Sir Hector Munro, lost his son.

The description of how young Munro died appeared in *The Gentleman's Magazine* in July 1793. An extract from the letter describes the attack on the young Englishman by a tiger on the Island of Saugor in the Sundarbans:

To describe the aweful, horrid and lamentable accident I have been an eye witness of, is impossible. Yesterday morning Mr Downey, of the Company's troops, (The East India Company), Lieut. Pyefinch, poor Mr Munro and myself went on shore on Saugor Island to shoot deer. We saw innumerable tracks of tigers and deer, but still we were induced to pursue our sport, and did the whole day. At about halfpast three we sat down on the edge of the jungle, to eat some cold meat sent us from the ship, and had just commenced our meal, when Mr Pyefinch and a black servant told us there was a fine deer within six yards of us. Mr Downey and myself immediately jumped up to take our guns; mine was the nearest, and I had just laid hold of it when I heard a roar, like thunder, and saw an immense tiger spring on the unfortunate Munro, who was sitting down. In a moment his head was in the beast's mouth, and he rushed into the jungle with him, with as much ease as I could lift a kitten, tearing him through the thickest bushes and trees, everything yielding to his monstrous strength. The agonies of horror, regret, and, I must say fear (for there were two tigers, male and female) rushed on me at once. The only effort I could make was to fire at him, though the poor youth was still in his mouth. I relied partly on Providence, partly on my own aim, and fired a musket. I saw the tiger stagger and agitated, and cried out so immediately. Mr Downey then fired two shots and I one more. We retired from the jungle, and, a few minutes after, Mr. Munro came up to us, all over blood, and fell. We took him on our backs to the boat, and got every medical assistance for him from the *Valentine* East India Man, which lay at anchor near the Island, but in vain. He lived twenty four hours in the extreme torture; his head and skull were torn and broke to pieces, and he was wounded by the claws all over the neck and shoulders; but it was better to take him away, though irrecoverable, than leave him to be devoured limb by limb. We have just read the funeral service over the body, and committed it to the deep. He was an amiable and promising youth. I must observe, there was a large fire blazing close to us, composed of ten or a dozen whole trees; I made it myself, on purpose to keep the tigers off, as I had always heard it would. There were eight or ten of the natives about us; many shots had been fired at the place, and much noise and laughing at the time; but this ferocious animal disregarded all. The human mind cannot form an idea of the scene; it turned my very soul within me. The beast was about four and a half feet high, and nine long. His head appeared as large as an ox's, his eyes darting fire, and his roar, when he first seized his prey, will never be out of my recollection. We had scarcely pushed our boats from the shore when the tigress made her appearance, raging mad almost, and remained on the sand as long as the distance would allow me to see her.[11]

When Tipu heard this story of young Munro's death it must have seemed to him to have been a just end: an infidel, the son of his enemy, eaten by the animal he most admired. The idea of capturing the scene forever in a splendid wooden statue must have appealed enormously to him. The man-tiger-organ is about half life size and depicts a wooden tiger mauling 'the wooden victim with his stylized red coat decorated with green and white roses, low crowned black hat, black knee breeches, white stockings and black shoes, was a British civilian.'[12] The victim's left hand moves up and down when the handle on the tiger's flank is turned. This also operates the bellows for the ingenious organ, which not only produces a limited range of notes but also reproduces the very real sound of the tiger growling in evident enjoyment as the European moans. The tiger itself is Indian in design but the intricate mechanism is thought to be French.

Tipu Sultan's obsessive hatred for the white man eventually led to his downfall. His treatment of the infidel prisoners and his blatant flaunting of treaties he made with them, gave the British the excuses they were looking for to attack. Tipu Sultan died defending his capital fortress at Seringapatam in 1799, fighting with the ferocity and courage of the animal he admired and revered, true confirmation of his right to the title of 'The Tiger of Mysore'.

The invaders found several tigers, the semi-pets of Tipu Sultan, chained in front of his quarters. Colonel Arthur Wellesley, later the Duke of Wellington, one of the commanders of the storming, wrote as a postscript to a letter to General Harris, the Supreme Commander: 'There are some tigers here, which I wish Meer Allum would send for, or else I must give orders to have them shot, as there is no food for them and nobody to attend to them, and they are getting violent.'[13] His fears were confirmed when a few days later:

a discharge of musketry was heard. Captain Price thinking the
populous had risen snatched up a bulse of diamonds which they
were registering and rushed to the door. There they saw six or
seven tigers scampering about and being fired upon by a party of
men from the 33rd Foot. Whether from the effect of the shot or a
convulsive effort by these formidable pets their moorings had
given way but after a few wild moments they were all destroyed, ... [one of them] giving his last roar actually at the side of
Price's palaquin. [14]

In the West and in India feelings against the tiger ran high, fuelled
by such emotive stories as the death of young Munro. The letter
quoted earlier was produced in various forms, even in children's
annuals, so instilling a deep fear of the tiger in children from a very
early age. Staffordshire potteries produced expensive chimney orna-
ments graphically depicting the scene with Munro's head in the jaws
of the tiger. The stories that filtered back to nineteenth century
England were exciting and uniformly anti-tiger. A picture of a hot,
distant country, seething with man-eating tigers, was firmly established in the minds and writings of those left at home. The stories
were always extreme: a bride snatched away from her husband's side
on the first night of their honeymoon or the 'little affecting anecdote
of the Hindoo mother, having her only child carried off by a tiger
while gathering fuel on the borders of the forest'. [15]

From now on the tiger was almost universally loathed as the
embodiment of the devil and the epitome of evil. He became a

Fig. 6   Arms of Lord Harris incorporating Tipu's fortress, Seringapatam

wicked and dangerous animal which should be exterminated at all costs, a point enlarged upon in later chapters. However, there were a few European artists and writers of the same era who saw beyond this popular image and still depicted the tiger as a magnificent beast with a noble form to be copied and admired.

7

Tiger with lithe and awesome grace
Delacroix

One of the first European painters to depict the tiger was the Englishman George Stubbs. He never condescended to his animal subjects but took a firm philosophical line. He believed they all had their own identity and individuality, were unique in their own right and totally independent of man, a view opposed by his critics who believed that artists should only set out to portray man's superiority over nature.

At the outset of his career Stubbs had made many exacting anatomical drawings of horses and humans. He enjoyed the grace and beauty, the mobile elegance and the sheer magnificence of his animal subjects. One of his earliest exhibits at the Society of Artists in 1764 was entitled 'A Tiger and a Lion'. He did not care to portray the ferocity of the tiger and the lion, killing or being killed, but was content to reproduce them in a calm and natural way.

The source for this tiger picture could well have been the Royal Menagerie at Windsor Great Park, for he had used a zebra from there the year before as the subject of another of his great works. The Duke of Cumberland certainly kept tigers at the Menagerie, not for any aesthetic or naturalistic reasons, but for matching with other animals in combat. Better known as Butcher Cumberland after his treatment of the Scots after the Battle of Culloden, this son of King George II matched his fine tiger against a stag in Windsor Great Park. Despite the enormous odds, the stag won, seriously wounding the tiger. The Duke was so impressed by the stag's courage and performance, he had a silver collar engraved with a record of the feat put round the animals neck and set it free.

Whatever the source of Stubbs's early paintings of a tiger, his last is exceptionally well documented. Towards the end of his life, in relative obscurity, he embarked on his final work, *The Comparative Anatomy of Humans, Chickens and Tigers*. The last subject came quite by chance for:

> at the time Mr Stubbs lived in Upper Seymour Street. Intelligence was brought him at ten o'clock in the evening that a dead tiger lay at Mr Pidcocks in the Strand, and it was obtainable at small expense if he thought proper to apply for it; his coat was hurried on, and he flew towards the well known place and presently entered the den where the dead animal lay extended: this was a precious moment; three guineas were given to the attendant, and the body was instantly conveyed to the painter's habitation, where in the place set apart for his muscular pursuits, Mr S. spent the rest of the night carbonading the once tremendous tyrant of the Indian jungle.[1] (plates 12 and 13)

There were a few errors in detail, the head being disproportionately small, due to a lack of perspective, which is strange for an artist of whom a critic had once said 'his tiger for grandeur has never been equalled'.[2]

The Mr Pidcock referred to was the owner of the Pidcocks Exhibition of Wild Beasts, a private menagerie in the Strand in London. There were also travelling menageries like the one that visited Newcastle in 1787. Thomas Bewick visited it and 'drew from life from a tiger exhibited in the city and was generally allowed to be one of the finest creatures of its kind ever seen in England.'[3] He used it as one of the illustrations in his book *A General History of Quadrupeds* published in 1790. His illustration, being first-hand, is certainly more accurate than his text which was heresay: 'The tiger is the most rapacious and destructive of all carnivorous animals. Fierce without provocation, and cruel without necessity, its thirst for blood is insatiable.' Possibly the tiger's keeper supplied the following to enhance his own position: 'The tiger is perhaps the only animal whose ferocity can never be subdued: neither gentleness nor constraint has any effect upon softening its temper. It does not seem sensible of the attention of its keeper; and would equally tear the hand that feeds with that by which it is chastised.'

Pidcocks was taken over to become Polito's Royal Menagerie and 'a constant visitor in 1816 was a curly headed youngster who was dividing his time between Polito's wild beasts at Exeter 'Change (off the Strand) and the Royal Academy Schools.[4] This fourteen-year-old boy was Edwin Landseer.

THE TIGER SELECTS A COW

AS THE TIGER SHOULDERS HIS VICTIM, THE ALARM IS CARRIED TO THE VILLAGE

THE VILLAGERS BEAT THE STRIP OF REED-GRASS

THE PICKED SPEARMEN OF THE VILLAGE STAND BEHIND THE NETS

THEY SPEAR THE TIGER AS HE STRUGGLES IN THE NET

40   Coloured engraving of Tipu Sultan on his tiger throne.

42   Tipu Sultan's banner bearing the inscription in Canarese: 'The Tiger is God'. The banner is on display at Windsor Castle

41   Tipu Sultan's sword with the unique 'tiger stripes' on the damascus blade

43   Bronze mortar cast in the form of a seated tiger found in Madras in 1838 but generally thought to have come from Tipu Sultan's arsenal at Seringapatam. It now stands in the Tower of the London Armoury

44   The carved tiger on the stock of one of Tipu Sultan's sporting guns, made at the royal arsenal at
Seringapatam. The stripes are inlaid with silver

45   The lock of one of Tipu Sultan's sporting guns. The chiselled steel cock in the shape of a tiger and the
tiny tiger safety-catch on its back illustrate well the lengths the 'Tiger of Mysore' went to in satisfying his passion
for tigers

46   This gruesome nineteenth century
Staffordshire earthenware figure of a tiger carrying off a
black boy typifies the feelings against the tiger in the
eighteenth and nineteenth century

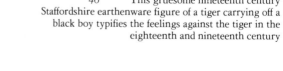

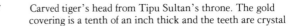

47   Carved tiger's head from Tipu Sultan's throne. The gold
covering is a tenth of an inch thick and the teeth are crystal

48   'Tigress Attacking a Bullock', A.D. 200. A Roman mosaic panel now in the well of the staircase in the Palazzo dei Conservatori, Rome

Landseer began his painting career at a time when the sombre classical style with its heavy intellectual approach was being superceded by the general move towards Romanticism. Taste veered away from faithful representation for with the rise of public menageries, the tiger was no longer an enigma. The public admired pictures of the magnificent and powerful animals, majestically set in their own surroundings, like Landseer's 'Monarch of the Glen'.

The fascination for mighty and dangerous animals was fired by the many travelling circuses and caged animal shows that now toured Britain and the Continent. People from all walks of life flocked to these performances where ferocious beasts, once so proud and free in the jungle, were made to perform tricks. One of the most popular animal acts was Isaac van Amburgh's performance with lions, tigers and leopards which could be seen at two London theatres, Astley's and Drury Lane. Sir Edwin Landseer recorded the scene and exhibited the painting at the Royal Academy in 1839; Queen Victoria thought it 'most beautiful... a wonderful piece of painting ... just exactly as I saw him'.[5] She in fact saw the performance at least five times. 'One can never see it too often,' she wrote in her Journal, 'for it is different each time... on the stage, at the same time, a lion & lioness, a tiger & 2 Chetas, or Kind of leopards. Van Amburgh remained about ¼ of an hour, showing them off & making them perform tricks. He has great power over the animals, & they seem to love him, though I think they are in great fear of him. He took them by their paws, throwing them down & making them roar, & he lay upon them after enraging them.'[6]

These menageries and travelling animal shows were obviously the only source of rare beasts for the European artists, just as the caged tigers in classical times inspired the brilliant mosaics found throughout the Roman Empire. In later times, when captive tigers were not available as live subjects, artists had to rely on earlier written descriptions of tigers to draw, sculpt or carve. Thus some are wildly inaccurate and scarcely recognizable as tigers. By the end of the eighteenth century, European artists – like those sponsored by the East India Company – were travelling to India to study live tigers at first-hand, although a few painters, like Zoffany, Thomas and William Daniell all of whom painted there, seemed more disposed to shoot their animal subjects than to paint them. However, Zoffany's tiger in 'The Death of the Royal Tyger' is a very strange beast (plate 56). He seems to have failed to make, or else lost, the proper sketches in India and relied solely on published illustrations in England for his subject. What is strange is that he did not paint a menagerie tiger like his contemporaries but most likely used the tiger from Conrad Gesner's *Icones Animalium* published in 1560 (plate 55). Comparison of the two tigers shows the identical dog-like head, the outsized claws and the inaccurate lion's tuft on the tail.

Le Jardin des Plantes, the famous botanical and zoological park in the centre of Paris, was an admirable source of tigers for *les Animaliers*, as the French animal painters of the nineteenth century were called.

Eugene Delacroix had visited Morocco and had seen lions in their natural surroundings but it was at *Le Jardin des Plantes* that he was able to study tigers at close quarters. Delacroix admired the animal's ferocity and was in total sympathy with his arrogant proud demeanour. He had no desire to exploit or belittle this mighty beast any more than he wished to decry its supposed cruelty. Apart from revelling in the more violent side of the tiger, a facet that mirrored his own inner feelings which he felt unable to express in life, he appreciated the aloofness and dignity of the feline spirit. This admiration is seen in his work, 'Tiger Playing with his Mother'.

Delacroix's friends commented that he even bore a remarkable resemblance to a tiger: 'he had tawny, feline eyes, with thick, arched brows, and a face of a wild and disconcerting beauty; yet he could be as soft as velvet, and could be stroked and caressed like one of those tigers whose lithe and awesome grace he excelled in portraying.'[7] Like Blake, Delacroix believed that men 'are tigers and wolves, bent on destroying one another'[8] which may account for his passion for depicting animals and men in fierce combat in which, for the first time in art, the outcome is uncertain (plate 53). He was a great admirer of his friend Antoine Louis Barye and would frequently sketch two small water-colours by him in the Louvre, declaring, 'I shall never be able to give the curl to a tiger's tail like that fellow can!'[9]

Antoine Louis Barye was of the same Romantic school as Delacroix, a school that 'was astonished and delighted by the accent of truth, liberty and sentiment of life therein'.[10] He, too, had great respect for the tiger which is clearly shown in his brilliant sculptures and paintings (plates 10 and 51). Each piece had a meticulous attention to anatomical detail which Barye, like his contemporaries, studied at *Le Jardin des Plantes*. When an old man, a visitor called at his house in the *Quai des Celestins* to find that Barye was out, Madame Barye smiled in explanation and said: 'Ah Monsieur, there is no use calling for at least three weeks. A new tiger has arrived from Bengal; until its wildness has gone – no Monsieur Barye!'[11]

Le Jardin des Plantes continued to be a source of inspiration to artists long after the nineteenth century school of Romanticism had died. However, it is more than likely that the tiger source also died in the Franco-Prussian war during the siege of Paris in 1871. Many, if not all, the animals were sold off for very high prices for food. The zoological side of the *Jardin* was restocked after the war and these animals, especially the tigers, were the subjects for many works by the great 'modern primitive' painter Henri Rousseau.

'Le Douanier' Rousseau (1844-1910) retired from his post as inspector in the Paris Municipal Toll at the age of forty to paint. His original, personal style was unhampered by the constraints of any formal training. The tiger was to become an important theme throughout his work and *'Tigre Poursuivant des Explorateurs'*, 'Tiger Pursued by Explorers', was one of the earliest works exhibited at the *Salon des Champs-Elysées*. Rousseau spent hours in *Le Jardin des Plantes*, sketching not only the wild animals in the zoological park but also the huge palms and flowers in the hot houses which held a particular fascination for him. These glimpses of a different, more exotic world flourished and crystallized in his imagination to re-appear, sometimes years later, as scenes of lush and brilliant jungles, crammed with flowers and oranges, snakes and monkeys and of course, the tiger.

Rousseau received little acclaim outside his immediate circle and little financial gain from his paintings during his lifetime. Indeed, *'Tempête dans la Jungle'*, 'Tropical Storm with a Tiger', was bought by Georges Courteline, a famous writer, to add to his collection 'a museum of horrors' (plate 54). Rousseau died in poverty but his paintings and primitive style with its unique quality of directness live and are admired throughout the world today.

Another caged tiger, itself a symbol of repressed wildness, was drawn from life at Copenhagen Zoo by Edvard Munch in 1909 (plate 50). Munch's subjects are haunting – a mixture of violent, often hysterical scenes, jealousy and sexuality. Intense neurotic emotionalism led to a nervous breakdown and his protracted visit to a clinic in Copenhagen. Human subjects were thought to be too upsetting for him but he was allowed to visit the zoo. There he drew, among all the other animals, the tiger, which must have been equally upsetting for him: a wild animal, caged, mirroring his inner torment. In a terse, masterly way he isolated the very nature of the animal, capturing it in a few strokes of the brush.

From these animal studies Munch produced 'Alpha and Omega', one of his most pessimistic works. It was a culmination of many of the themes of his pictures; love, jealousy, the faithlessness of women, melancholia, anxiety and death. 'The Tiger' is just one part of this parody of Adam and Eve, 'The tiger put its cruel wild head against Omega's lovely little face. Omega did not tremble. She put her hand into the tiger's mouth, and stroked its teeth.'[12]

Everyone has their own view of the tiger. To Tipu Sultan he was the model for his life, to the ancient Greeks and Romans a rarity to be revered. To the owners of the early menageries the tiger was a symbol of power over nature or an object of amusement when pitted against other animals. To the many artists who portrayed him the tiger took many roles; Stubbs admired his independence, Delacroix and Barye his energy, while to Rousseau he was simply exotic, and to Munch he was the wild animal, caged, restrained against his will, representing his own frustration. To William Blake, the tiger was an enigma, symbolizing the combination of good and evil, of God and the devil.

The Tiger

Tiger! Tiger! burning bright
In the forests of the night,
What immortal hand or eye
Could frame thy fearful symmetry?

In what distant deeps or skies
Burned the fire of thine eyes?
On what wings dare he aspire?
What the hand dare seize the fire?

And what shoulder, and what art,
Could twist the sinews of thy heart?
And when thy heart began to beat,
What dread hand? And what dread feet?

What the hammer? What the chain?
In what furnace was thy brain?
What the anvil? What dread grasp
Dare its deadly terrors clasp?

When the stars threw down their spears,
And watered heaven with their tears,
Did he smile his work to see?
Did he who made the Lamb make thee?

Tiger! Tiger! burning bright
In the forests of the night,
What immortal hand or eye
Dare frame thy fearful symmetry?[13]

8

The mark of Wang, King of the Beasts
Chalmers Werner

Since the earliest civilizations, many properties both good and evil, real and apocryphal, have been attributed to the tiger. These properties have had far reaching effects on many cultures and ideas throughout the whole of the tiger's range and in the Western world. Whatever the general feeling towards the tiger at the time, he has always been a symbol of power, be it malign, or one to be emulated and harnessed for good. The form this symbol of power takes has varied within each culture and era. It embraces many subjects, from a whole civilization to the luck of the gambler, from religion to advertising, from military might to a loveable character animal.

To Western eyes India and the tiger are synonymous. As early as 2000 BC the tiger was chosen as the emblem of one of the world's first civilizations in the north-west of India. The Aryans from Mohenjo Daro obviously appreciated the tiger for his powerful qualities, judging by the number of tiger seals found on the site. To the Western cartoonists India has always been symbolized as the tiger, like the British lion or the French cockerel. In fact the lion, not the tiger, was the national emblem of India, but comparatively recently the tiger was reinstated after nearly 4,000 years. There was, of course, one Indian province in the eighteenth century that adopted the tiger as its emblem and that was Mysore. Tipu Sultan not only took the tiger to symbolize his regime but to symbolize the Muslim faith. The Muslim tiger devouring the Hindu bird was a common motif during the many religious wars (plate 60).

The tiger is not a biblical animal, but he does appear in prayer books and other religious works. In the 1585 Thanksgiving Liturgy Service a prayer asks, 'to save her [Queen Elizabeth] from the jaws of

the cruel tigers that then sought to suck her blood'.[1] Another
reference to the tiger from a religious poem of about the same date:
'Thou hes Blaspheminist our Prophet, Priest, and heid; O filthie
tegre of Babylonical'[2] exactly illustrates the measure of Tudor England's regard for the tiger. Using the tiger as a symbol of evil and an
object of fear was by no means an original idea. Two centuries earlier
Chaucer twice described the tiger as a demonic and fickle beast in his
'Squire's Tale': he first mentioned the tiger as 'ne noon so crueel a
beast', and, later, a bird alludes to her false lover as '...this tigre ful
of doubleness'.[3] Such deceit was a common charge against the tiger
in the Middle Ages, usually associated with women.

In *The Third Part of King Henry the Sixth*, Shakespeare uses this
duplicity in a speech by the Duke of York in vilifying Queen
Margaret on hearing that his son had been murdered. Already
branding Queen Margaret as 'the she wolf of France', York continues:

> O tiger's heart wrapp'd in a woman's hide!
> How couldst thou drain the life-blood of the child,
> To bid the father wipe his eyes withal,
> And yet be seen to bear a woman's face?

Adding treachery to the tiger's list of evils, Shakespeare uses Pliny's
reference to tigers to press home York's message:

> But you are more inhuman, more inexorable –
> O, ten times more – than tigers of Hyrcania.[4]

Not surprisingly, it is in military contexts that the fierce and fearless
qualities of the tiger are extolled. In Shakespeare's *King Henry the
Fifth* the lines delivered by the King before the walls of the French
fortress, Harfleur, illustrate the regard in which the tiger was held:

> Once more unto the breach, dear friends, once more;
> Or close the wall up with our English dead.
> In peace there's nothing so becomes a man
> As modest stillness and humility;
> But when the blast of war blows in our ears,
> Then imitate the action of the tiger:
> Stiffen the sinews, summon up the blood,
> Disguise fair nature with hard-favour'd rage;[5]

The symbol of the tiger for military power, strength and courage was much used by the Chinese. *Shuo Wen*, a dictionary from the Han Dynasty (206BC-AD220) refers to 'an auspicious jade of tiger design, used to mobilize an army' (plate 20). Clearly they wished to emulate their symbol, as for centuries their elite troops were dressed in tiger uniforms (plate 29) striped with tiger ears and tails. *Shuo Wen* describes how they would advance into battle 'shouting loudly in the hope that their cries would strike terror into the enemy, as if they were the actual roars of the tiger'. Tiger charms were issued to the troops to instil courage and fierceness in battle. Considering the importance the Chinese military placed on the image of the tiger, it is surprising that it was only the insignia of an officer of the fourth class and not of the supreme commander.

In the British Army the tiger insignia was adopted by many regiments. Some of these regiments were originally raised by the East India Company, e.g. the Royal Dublin Fusiliers and the Royal Munster Fusiliers who later gained a considerable reputation for 'fighting like tigers' during the Indian Mutiny. Other regiments, like the West Yorkshire, the Yorkshire and Lancashire, the Hampshire, the Leicestershire and the Gordon Highlanders adopted the Bengal tiger as their insignia after serving in India.

Individuals too, incorporated the tiger into their coats of arms, initially as a symbol of courage and ferocity but later to signify some connection with the East. The early tiger crests portrayed a very different beast from the later, more accurate ones. The heraldic 'Tyger' had a lion's body, no stripes, tufts about the ears and mane, curious tusks, a pointed beak on the end of his nose and the tufted tail of a lion. This tiger was of no use to those who had seen the real animal and so the Bengal tiger was introduced into heraldry.

The tiger also represents authority. Early Chinese ambassadors were sent on their missions with a *hu chieh*, a tiger stick, as the symbol of their authority. Magistrates sat on tiger skins to show their power and to intimidate the defendants, and tiger screens were evident at the entrance to the court. Professors, soldiers and heroes all sat on tiger skins, *kao-pi*, to suggest that they would leave their learning and greatness to posterity in the same way that the tiger left behind his beautiful skin. In China, the tiger has also been a symbol of good luck. A gambling hall would often display a portrait or a statue of a tiger with a sack of money or gold between his paws or in his mouth. Incense or food offerings were placed before 'His Excellency the cash-grasping tiger' on the second and sixteenth days of each month.

Perhaps this 'tiger of chance' lent his name to the American game of faro where to 'buck the tiger' is to take the bank. Referring to this, one Chicago newspaper claimed that 'more than one unsuspecting wife will have had her eyes opened to the fact that the wicked tiger, and not legitimate business has been detaining her husband out so late at night'.[6]

In the modern field of advertising 'tiger power' is credible. In the imagination of the buyer every product associated with the tiger adopts the qualities of that animal. A soap powder with 'tiger power' kills dirt quickly and ruthlessly, tiger balm spirits pain away, tiger matches burn brighter, tiger beer is stronger, tiger petrol more powerful.

Unquestionably the single most successful advertising compaigns using the tiger are those of Esso Petroleum. These started in the early 1950s when Esso introduced a ferocious, leaping tiger to advertise their top grade of petrol. The symbol was so popular that public demand would not allow Esso to drop it. In the mid 1960s Esso launched their whimsical, cartoon tiger accompanied by the slogan 'Put a Tiger in your Tank!' It had simplicity: its symbol conveyed a single message, power. The Esso tiger became a 'folk hero' throughout the world. He spoke practically every language, his smiling face and roar were loved in every continent. The public were reluctant to let 'their' tiger go, but he was finally phased out in 1969. The massive campaign cost millions to mount but Esso's sales graph rose correspondingly. This cartoon character did much to soften the image of the tiger.

With the world shortage of fossil fuels, the advertising accent has been switched to minimum use of energy for maximum output. Today the Esso tiger has a new role, it has become the symbol for economy of movement combined with efficiency and power. The tiger is also symbolic of Esso's success in the North Sea. Leaping out of the sea, compact, muscled, controlled, tense with power, the tiger can be seen from hoardings throughout Europe as well as on commerical television.

'Tiger power' was even harnessed by the gods. Shiva, the Hindu god of destruction and regeneration, was clad in a tiger skin and rode on a tiger (plate 57). When cow worship superceded tiger worship, Shiva was demoted to a bullock but kept his clothes and a tiger skin saddle cloth. His wife, Durga the Inaccessible, also rode a tiger. With her mount and ten arms brandishing swords, she must have been invincible.

The Greek god Dionysus (the Roman Bacchus) was frequently portrayed 'beneath a thickly spreading vine ... accompanied by Silenus and riding a chariot drawn by two tigresses and led by a satyr' (plate 58).[7] Here the god is flaunting his triumph over mere mortals by harnessing nature. Martial (AD40-104), author of the great collection of epigrams or short stories, compares the Roman Emperor Domitianus, victor of the Samatian wars with Dionysus: 'too many tigers drew your chariots into the arena, compared with Dionysus and India where he was content with only two tigers to draw him'. Martial uses the same comparison with Claudius I:

> The robber in the East by the banks of the Ganges, pale with fear on his Hyrcanian mount, did not dread as many tigresses as your Rome ... Your arena shows Caesar has outdone the Eastern triumphs of the victor god and all his wealth; for when Bacchus drove captive Indians beneath his yoke he was content with only two tigresses to draw him.[8]

Tiger-riding was not confined to the gods and ancients as the lady of Riga found to her cost:

> There was a young lady of Riga,
> Who rode with a smile on a tiger,
> They returned from the ride
> With the lady inside
> And the smile on the face of the tiger.[9]

The changing attitudes towards the tiger are reflected in the tiger's treatment in children's stories. Up to the turn of the twentieth century the tiger was always the symbol of fear, the foreign 'big bad wolf'. The tiger's treachery invariably resulted in his death, usually macabre and unpleasant. Stories like *Little Black Sambo* delighted Victorian children. There the wicked tigers stole the boy's new clothes and chased themselves so fast round a tree that they melted. Every animal in Kipling's anthropomorphic *Jungle Book* is a friend to the boy Mowgli except the tiger, Sher Khan. A complete outcast, Sher Khan is finally killed by the boy and skinned. The cartoon strip and comic *Tiger Tim* portrayed the tiger in a slightly more sympathetic light, paving the way for A. A. Milne's loveable Tigger in *Winnie the Pooh*. He is bright and eternally optimistic, but, in contrast to the other characters, Tigger is also brash and gaudy, the unclassifiable foreigner who does not know the rules. Today too many children's stories portray the tiger as a soft character, rather like an overgrown ginger cat, far removed from reality.

The tiger has been greatly admired down the centuries as a magnificent beast, a mighty hunter, an animal renowned for its speed and courage. But perhaps the part of him which has most impressed man has been his amazing striated, striped and barred pelt with its superb colouring; it is his skin that hunters prize.

Fig. 7   Tigger from *Winnie the Pooh*

The tiger's colouring has caused his name to be lent to many other species: butterflies, moths, beetles and flowers. There are dozens of butterflies and moths that have 'tiger' colouring. The Jersey Tiger, *Euplagia quadripunctaria*, either with red or yellow background has the required black stripes and spots. It is quite common throughout south-west England and, strangely, in Butterfly Valley on the island of Rhodes in Greece where they hatch on the same day and take off· literally in clouds. The Swallow Tail butterfly has the most striking 'tiger' markings but, surprisingly, none of its several sub-species are known by tiger names. The Plain Tiger, *Danaus chrysippus*, is another dramatic example of a tiger-striped British butterfly. Tiger moths, *Arctiidæ*, are very common throughout Britain and have different coloured backgrounds but always the regulation black spots. The Wood Tiger is one of the most handsome. Tiger beetles, *Cinin-deladæ*, are very common throughout the tropical world. Again it is their tiger colouring that gives them their name. Flowers too bear the tiger's name like the ubiquitous tiger lilly, *lilium tigrinium*, that black speckled flower that should not be confused with the re-doubtable *Tigerlillia terribilis* discovered by Edward Lear towards the end of the last century:

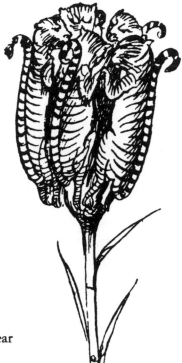

Fig. 8   *Tigerlillia terribilis* by Edward Lear

It was the amazing stripes and bars which made the tiger's skin so special. Not surprisingly the pelt was the prized trophy of the hunter. Like Mowgli in *The Jungle Book* the hunter should 'know better than anyone else how an animal's skin is fitted on, and how it should be taken off'[10]. Having shot the tiger, great care was taken by the hunter in the skinning. The tiger was laid on his back and slit from his lower lip down to the tip of the tail, then from the pads, evenly down the white of the legs to the central cut, taking care not to cut the flesh. The coat was then simply stripped off the body. Finally the skin was pegged out in the shade, starting at the head and tail to get the maximum length and followed by the sides and legs. Any fat tissue or flesh was scraped off before a mixture of alum and saltpetre was rubbed into the reverse of the skin.

The skins so treated, perhaps with some further attention from a taxidermist, were then ready to adorn the home of the hunter as a symbol of his prowess or to be exported throughout the world. One such has been immortalized by Elinor Glyn in her novel *Three Weeks*, where the heroine is the recipient of a magnificent tiger skin:

> Paul entered from the terrace. And the loveliest sight of all, in front of the fire, stretched at full length, was his tiger [skin] and on him – also at full length – reclined the lady, ... one white arm resting on the beast's head ... She was evidently in the Devil's mood.
>
> 'No! You must not come near me, Paul .. Not yet. You brought me the tiger. Ah that was good! My beautiful tiger!' And she gave a movement like a snake, of joy to feel its fur under her, while she stretched out her hands and caressed the creature where the hair turned white and black at the side, and was deep and soft.
>
> 'Beautiful one! Beautiful one!' she purred. 'And I know all your feelings and your passions, and now I have got your skin – for the joy of my skin.' And she quivered again with a movement of a snake. [11] (plate 49)

The novel – in particular this tiger skin scene – was thought highly scandalous in 1907, which is probably why it sold two million copies all over the world in countless languages. Inevitably Elinor Glyn was linked with her fictional heroines, all passionate, promiscuous and beautiful and it was only a matter of time before the following rhyme became popular:

> Would you like to sin
> with Elinor Glyn
> on a tiger skin?
> Or would you prefer
> to err
> with her
> on some other fur? [12]

The more fashionable furriers perferred to leave the tiger skins as rugs and trophies. The pelt is too coarse and tough to make an elegant full length coat, although there was a vogue for tiger skin created by Dior in the 1960s in France. However, tiger skin has been used throughout the ages for trimmings. At Shrovetide, just before Lent, in 1509 a masked ball was held at Richmond where King Henry VIII appeared in a Russian dress of fur while the Princess Mary, later Queen Mary Tudor, wore a 'black mask as an Ethopian Queen and a little jacket of tiger skin'. [13] Possibly the earlier furriers

had the same opinion of tiger pelts as their successors judging from
the scores of references for practically every other fur but the tiger's.
Today most countries in the world have banned the importation of
tiger skins and, although there are still a few women who wear tiger
skins and still some houses with old trophies and tiger skin rugs on
display, most remaining skins have been banished to the attics in
embarrassment.

As fast as the tiger was being promoted throughout the world
through advertising and children's writings, the real animal was
disappearing off the face of the earth. It would indeed be a tragedy if
the tiger was only remembered as the animal who lent his name to
other species who share his brilliant, striated markings and his
ferocity.

9
Shikar!
Jim Corbett

Whatever the feeling towards, or the portrayal of, the tiger throughout history it is his death that invokes the most reaction. The war against the tiger was firmly established by the ruling classes throughout the whole of the tiger's range by the middle of the eighteenth century. The fabulously wealthy maharajas and nawabs of India were soon emulated by the military and civilian officers of the East India Company who took to tiger hunting with a vengeance. They in turn were replaced by the officers of the Indian Army, the visiting British regiments and the thousands in government service. It became expected for a young subaltern to prove himself by shooting at least one tiger, just as it was obligatory for a local maharajah to lay on a tiger hunt for a visiting dignitary.

The actual method of hunting tigers for sport varied with the type of country and the finances of the hunter. To hunt in the dense jungles of Assam or Nepal or the *terai* forests of the Himalayan foothills, the hunter needed elephants. In the more open country of southern and central India a line of native beaters were used to flush out the tiger and drive him past the hunters who lay safely concealed behind rocks. The most common and inexpensive method was to sit over a bait, like a tethered bullock or a fresh tiger kill, in a *machán* or tree hide and wait until the tiger appeared.

One of the earliest accounts of a grand tiger hunt with elephants was written by Sir John Day in a letter dated April 1784 to his friend Sir William Jones. The hunt took place on the banks of the Ganges in Bengal. John Zoffany was one of the hunters and used an identical hunt a little later for his painting 'The Death of the Royal Tyger' completed in 1788 (plate 56).

Matters had been thus judiciously arranged: tents were sent off yesterday, and an encampment formed within a mile and a half of the jungle which was to be the scene of our operations; and in this jungle the thickets of long rank grass and reeds are in many places fifteen feet high. At one o'clock this morning thirty elephants, with the servants, and refreshments of all kinds, were dispatched; at two we all followed in fly-palaquins [a covered litter]; at a quarter to four we reached the encampment, and having rested near two hours, we mounted our elephants, and proceeded to the jungle.

In our way we met with game of all kinds: hares, antelope, hog-deer, wild boars and wild buffaloes; but nothing could divert our attention from the fiercer and more glorious game.

At the grey of the dawn we formed a line of great extent, and entered a small detached jungle. My elephant, (sorely against my grain, but there was no remedy for my driver was a keen sports-man and he and I spoke no common language) passed through the centre, but happily no tiger had at that hour nestled there. I saw, however, as I passed through it, the bed of one, in which there were an half devoured bullock and two human skulls; with a heap of bones, some bleached, and some still red with gore.

We had not proceeded five hundred yards beyond the jungle, when we heard a general cry on our left of '*Baug, baug, baug*!' On hearing this exclamation of 'tiger!' we wheeled; and forming a line anew, entered the great jungle, when the spot where a single tiger lay having been pointed, on the discharge of the first gun a scene presented itself confessed by all the experienced tiger hunters present to be the finest they had ever seen. Five full grown royal tigers sprung together from the same spot, where they had sat in bloody congress. They ran diversely; but running heavily they all couched again within new covers within the same jungle, and all were marked. We followed, having formed a line into a crescent, so as to embrace either extremity of the jungle: in the centre was the houdar (or state) elephants, with the marksmen, and the ladies, to comfort and encourage them.

When we had slowly and warily approached the spot where the first tiger lay, he moved not until we were just upon him; when, with a roar that resembled thunder, he rushed upon us. The elephants wheeled off at once and shuffled off. They returned, however, after a flight of about fifty yards, and again approaching the spot where the tiger had lodged himself, towards the skirts of the jungle, he once more rushed forth, and springing at the side of an elephant upon which three of the natives were mounted, at one stroke tore a portion of the pad from under them; and one of the riders, panic struck, fell off. The tiger, however seeing his enemies in force, returned, slow and indignant, into his shelter; where, the place he lay in being marked, a heavy and well directed fire was poured in by the principal marksman; when, pushing in, we saw him in the struggle of death, and growling and foaming he expired.

We then proceeded to seek the others, having first distinguished the spot by pitching a tall spear, and tying to the end of it the muslin of a turban. We roused four in close succession, and with a little variation of circumstances, killed them all; the oldest and most ferocious of the family, had, however, early in the conflict, very sensibly quitted the scene of action, and escaped to another part of the country.

While the fate of the last and largest was depending, more shots were fired than in the three other attacks; he escaped four several assaults, and taking posts in different parts of the jungle, rushed upon us at each wound he received with a kindled rage, and as often put the whole line to flight. In the last pursuit he singled out the elephant upon which Lady Day was; and was at its tail, with jaws distended and in the act of rising upon his hind paws to fasten on her, when fortunately she cleared the jungle; and a great discharge from the hunters having forced him to give up the chase, he returned to his shelter. The danger, I believe, was not very great; but it was sufficient, when she shall be invited again, to make her say with Lord Chesterfield, when they attempted to allure him to a second fox hunt, 'I have been.'

The chase being over, we returned in triumph to our encampment, and we were followed by the spoils of the morning, and by an accumulating multitude of the peasants from the circumjacent villages, who pressed round an open tent in which we sat at breakfast, with congratulations, blessings and thanksgivings. The four tigers were laid in front, the natives viewed them with terror, and some with tears.

An old woman, looking earnestly at the largest tiger, and pointing at times to his tusks, and at times lifting his forepaws, and viewing his talons, her furrows bathed in tears, in broken and moaning tones narrated something to a little circle composed of three Brahmins and a young woman with a child in her arms. No human misery could pierce the phlegm and apathy of the Brahmins, and with them there was not a feature softened; but horror and sorrow were alternatively painted in the face of the female;

and, from her clasping at times her child more closely to her breast, I guessed the subject of the old woman's story, and upon inquiry I found that I was right in my conjecture. She was widowed and childless; she owed both her misfortunes to the tigers of that jungle, and most probably to those which then lay dead before her, for they, it was believed, had recently carried off her husband and her two sons grown up to manhood, and now she wanted food; in the phrenzy of her grief she alternately described her loss to the crowd, and in a wild scream demanded her husband and her children from the tigers; indeed it was a piteous spectacle!

The site of our encampment was well chosen; it was a small sloping lawn, the verdure fresh, and skirted on three sides with trees; the fourth bounded by the deep bed of a torrent river. At proper distances on this lawn, there were five large and comodious tents, pitched in a semicircle: that in which we all assembled, and passed the sultry part of the day, was carpeted, and by means of the tattees of aromatic grass, continually watered, kept at a temperature pretty near to that of an April day in England. Here we had a luxurious cold dinner, with a variety of excellent wines, and other liquors, well cooled; and while we dined, the French horns and clarionets played marches, hunting pieces descriptive of the death of the game, and other slow movements; the tigers still lying in front, and the people still assembled, but retired to a greater distance; where they anxiously waited for the signal for skinning and cutting up the slain; for with them the fat of the tiger is a panacea, the tongue dried and pulverised a sovereign specific in nervous cases, and every part applicable to some use, even the whiskers they deem a deadly poison, and most anxiously, but secretly, seek them, as a means, in drink, of certain destruction to an enemy.

Dinner over, the tigers skinned, and the flesh and offal distributed, as soon as the sun declined we returned to Chinsura; and here ends the history of the chase. [1]

This account is typical of a fairly grand tiger hunt of its day, although it varies little from those of the Mogul Emperors Babar, Aurangzeb, Akbar the Great or Jehangir who hunted with bows and arrows and spears from horses and elephants with their companions. Equally this account could very nearly suffice for any other tiger hunt during the nineteenth century and from then on up to the eventual ban on hunting in 1970. The size of the bag, the numbers killed or wounded and their length and weight became increasingly important in the nineteenth century and as firearms improved the odds became heavily loaded against the tiger. These 'sportsmen' were not the only threat to the tiger as tigers attracted both European bounty hunters like Captain Cauldfield and native slayers who resorted to poison. They would find a fresh kill and cut long gashes in the flesh into which they rubbed strychnine, arsenic or the local poison from some jungle berry which when eaten by the tiger, caused a lingering death. The bounty from such a kill was often worth several months salary.

To Europeans, tiger hunting became an obsession. One of the most prolific hunters of the Victorian era was George Yule of the Bengal Civil Service. When his tally after twenty-five years reached 400 he did not bother to record the others he killed. Colonel Rice, the author of several works on tiger hunting, killed and wounded 93 tigers between 1850 and 1854. Another author/sportsman, George Cumming, shot 73 while Montague Gerard had accounted for 227 in central India and Hyderabad by 1903.

These 'bags' of the British Army and civilian officers were small compared with the fabulously rich maharajas and nawabs. The record for all time is that of the Maharaja of Surguja at 1,150. The Maharaja Scindia accounted for over 700 and his guests a further 200. The former Prime Minister of Nepal killed 295 tigers in seven years from 1933 and many others 'scored' over a century like the Maharajas Udaipur, Kotah and Jaipur.

The size of the tiger was almost as important as the number shot. Skins were stretched when pegged out on the ground to give more impressive records but any tiger over ten feet, between pegs, was a respectable size and those at eleven feet were records for their area. The Raja of Gauripur claimed an eleven foot tiger and over a dozen at record size, over ten feet, out of his total of over 500.

In central and southern India, where the country is more open than in the north and there are fewer elephants, the tiger was hunted 'on foot'. The tiger was not actually stalked as the term supposes but driven by a line of beaters on foot towards the guns positioned on some high vantage point like a tree, rock or bank. The high position was chosen not only for safety but also because a driven tiger will not look up, so the hunter, or *shikar*, can stay concealed and have a wider angle of fire.

Instructions for such a tiger shoot are given by Colonel William Rice, writing in 1857:

Having collected the required number of men and the likeliest cover the hunter would start off for his post with two men carrying the spare guns and water bag... On arrival at the spot where he was to wait in ambush, these two men would be sent back silently to join the rest of the beaters and tell them that all was ready to begin...

To enable the men beating the covers to make as much noise as possible they were provided with four kettle drums, called *tansees*, made of tin with a goat's skin tightly braced over the top. These instruments, struck with a short cane, emitted a most discordant noise.

A big bell was also provided, which made as much row as any dinner bell. This was intended to imitate the bells often worn round the necks of elephants belonging to the native chiefs who occasionally got up hunting parties among these jungles...My own *Shikarrees* were entrusted with a pair of old horse pistols and a horn each filled with coarse gunpowder with which they fired blank shots at intervals. These repeated shots greatly encouraged the beaters, for they knew no large game would wait for them to almost step upon when it heard such frequent shots coming onwards...

The villagers had their own drawn swords, bows and arrows and short spears...Stones were flung or thrown with wonderful force and aimed into every likely looking bush and were most useful for starting any tiger that might be disposed to lurk too long in cover or refuse to move at all as sometimes happened...

All the men were directed to keep always in as compact a body as possible, no straggling, and to make their utmost yelling, which they certainly did with a will. This procession, which always moved very slowly and carefully, was called the 'band'. There was not the slightest danger to anyone taking part in such a movement, for the din was so great that no animal likes waiting for it...

Now all being in readiness the 'band' strikes up an aweful din, while some single blank pistol shots are at once fired for safety's sake. The moment the aweful row commences it is most curious to note the sudden change from the perfect stillness that reigns in the jungle in the mid-day heat. Clouds of green parrots, wood pigeons also green doves in swarms, a large horned owl or two and pea fowl in numbers come sweeping by in the greatest alarm. Monkeys, the large grey hoonuman, begin to call their 'hoop, hoop' noise, to be soon changed to their other note of alarm, the loud, husky, repeated cough or swearing as it sounds like, should either tiger or panther be afoot... peacocks are found in great number, and they are very useful indeed for the hunter can tell if either tiger or panther is about...

Nothing can be finer than to watch these grand peacocks viewed from above on the steep sides of the ravine. As they skim along in their flight, the sun shining on their long tails they seem to leave a lengthened quivering wave of light in their wake for scores will be seen gliding past, a truly splendid sight.

Presently the distant din becomes more audible, the 'band' has turned the corner of the ravine, and now is heard the double shots of the horse pistol with perhaps the loud sudden 'wough' of the tiger, startled by the dreadful row from some shady retreat that he had intended to lie up in, letting the beaters pass, but now he finds he must break forward. This in the middle of the hot weather is no joke, for the burning sands and stones, ... will blister if stood on for half a minute, and have to be passed over, not to mention the annoyance of being wakened from sleep, so naturally the beast is in a vicious state of rage and fright combined. On he comes at a steady trot ... keeping no very sharp look out.

It now behoves the sportsman to keep as quiet as possible, not moving a finger even, and if the rifle has to be cocked it must be done noiselessly without jerking the gun barrels for the tiger's hearing and vision on these occasions are both most acute; the glimmer of a gun moving being especially liable to attract his attention. Of course the hunter will have taken care to have his dress in a uniform brown colour, without any white or any conspicuous shining objects about him, his hat being the same dark green colour, while all signs or white collars or shirts are quite invisible. All these precautions are indispensible, or the animal instead of coming properly on and so affording a steady killing shot, will bound back with a roar very likely, and at a pace that makes hitting very doubtful ...

On hearing the hunters' shots and the loud 'wough wough!' that is sure to be pumped out on his being fired at for, hit or not, in his rage this angry grunt is sure to be uttered, the men should be instructed to redouble, if possible, their previous din which they are luckily almost sure to do of their own accord, for this extra noise will prevent a confused wounded tiger having any idea of trying to bolt back again as well as perhaps to start forward a second beast or more should they be in the same cover ...

Now as to where to fire at the passing or already passed tiger – if it is a slow-creeping cautious brute within reasonable distance say twenty to thirty yards, a good rifle shot will kill it dead by a ball through the head or ear, and so save further trouble, a tiger's brain being comparatively small, and lies in a long narrow cell at the extreme top of the skull. Under the forearm, half way up the breadth of the body is not bad, for this goes through the lungs and soon disables the brute; care must be taken not to hit the shoulder which is thick and muscular but decidedly the best shot and the easiest to fire at what will break the liver; this is a large mark quite eight inches round about half way down, a third of the way up the animal's body.

Now comes the worst part of the hunt, for unless a good or lucky shot has left the tiger dead on the ground it must be followed up again until either found dead or alive. These kills at once are seldom, about one in five.[2]

By deliberately wounding the tiger in the name of 'sport' the *shikar* had made his victim extremely dangerous. Great, but necessary, courage was needed to follow up on foot and most fatal or serious accidents happened at this stage of the hunt (plate 64). The hunter following up a wounded tiger was advised to keep his eyes

> not on the tracks or trail but in the cover ahead where the beast is likely to lie concealed. If the tiger charges, as it will in most cases if still possessing the ability to do so, do not fire too soon, ... a shot fired at twenty or thirty yards may fail and leave an empty barrel and one chance the less.[3]

The advice was easily given but difficult to follow as the furious tiger, roaring as it charged, could cover that distance in under two seconds. Sometimes a herd of buffalo was used as 'pointers' as the buffalo would split when approaching a tiger. This never really worked and was dangerous for the herdsman if the tiger charged over the backs of the buffalo.

Even after the tiger had been 'killed' there were still dangers as a Madras sepoy found to his cost while measuring a tiger that was supposed to be dead, for it suddenly struck him and fractured his skull with one blow of 'the mighty paw'. One officer, who was also severely mauled 'did not know whether his wounds were very dangerous, so before they became stiff he rode twenty-four miles back to Surat'. He was very weak from loss of blood, but a 'glass of sherry cocked his tail again'![4]

The last and most common way that tigers were shot was from a *machán* over a live, tethered bait or a fresh tiger kill (plate 30). The bait was usually a young buffalo calf, but sometimes a smaller domestic animal, like a goat, was used. The more insensitive hunters would put pepper in their bait's eyes to make them bleat louder to make certain they would attract a tiger.

One of the best descriptions of shooting from a *machán* is by Saki and called 'Mrs Packletide's Tiger'. No apology is given for reproducing it in full as a piece of light relief from the other descriptions of tiger slaughter. Saki's real name was H. H. Munro and he was the direct descendant of Sir Hector Munro, the successful adversary of Tipu Sultan.[5]

It was Mrs Packletide's pleasure and intention that she should shoot a tiger. Not that the lust to kill had suddenly descended on her, or that she felt that she would leave India safer and more wholesome than she had found it, with one fraction less of wild beast per million inhabitants. The compelling motive for her sudden deviation towards the footsteps of Nimrod was the fact that Loona Bimberton had recently been carried eleven miles in an aeroplane by an Algerian aviator, and talked of nothing else; only a personally procured tiger-skin and a heavy harvest of Press photographs could successfully counter that sort of thing. Mrs Packletide had already arranged in her mind the lunch she would give at her house in Curzon Street, ostensibly in Loona Bimberton's honour, with a tiger-skin rug occupying most of the foreground and all of the conversation. She had also already designed in her mind the tiger-claw brooch that she was going to give Loona Bimberton on her next birthday [plate 61]. In a world that is supposed to be chiefly swayed by hunger and by love, Mrs Packletide was an exception; her movements and motives were largely governed by dislike of Loona Bimberton.

Circumstances proved propitious. Mrs. Packletide had offered a thousand rupees for the opportunity of shooting a tiger without overmuch risk or exertion, and it so happened that a neighbouring village could boast of being the favoured rendezvous of an animal of respectable antecedents, which had been driven by the increasing infirmities of age to abandon game-killing and confine its appetite to the smaller domestic animals. The prospect of earning the thousand rupees had stimulated the sporting and commercial instinct of the villagers; children were posted night and day on the outskirts of the local jungle to head the tiger back in the unlikely event of his attempting to roam away to fresh hunting-grounds, and the cheaper kinds of goats were left about with elaborate carelessness to keep him satisfied with his present quarters. The one great anxiety was lest he should die of old age before the date appointed for the memsahib's shoot. Mothers carrying their babies home through the jungle after the day's work in the fields hushed their singing lest they might curtail the restful sleep of the venerable herd-robber.

The great night duly arrived, moonlit and cloudless. A platform had been constructed in a comfortable and conveniently placed tree and thereon crouched Mrs Packletide and her paid companion, Miss Mebbin. A goat, gifted with a particularly persistent bleat, such as even a partially deaf tiger might be reasonably expected to hear on a still night, was tethered at the correct distance. With an accurately sighted rifle and a thumb-nail pack of patience cards the sportswoman awaited the coming of the quarry.

'I suppose we are in some danger?' said Miss Mebbin.

She was not actually nervous about the wild beast, but she had a morbid dread of performing an atom more service than she had been paid for.

'Nonsense,' said Mrs Packletide; 'it's a very old tiger. It couldn't spring up here even it it wanted to.'

'If it's an old tiger I think you ought to get it cheaper. A thousand rupees is a lot of money.'

Louisa Mebbin adopted a protective elder-sister attitude towards money in general, irrespective of nationality or denomination. Her energetic intervention had saved many a rouble from dissipating itself in tips in some Moscow hotel, and francs and centimes clung to her instinctively under circumstances which would have driven them headlong from less sympathetic hands. Her speculations as to the market depreciation of tiger remnants were cut short by the appearance on the scene of the animal itself. As soon as it caught sight of the tethered goat it lay flat on the earth, seemingly less from a desire to take advantage of all available cover than for the purpose of snatching a short rest before commencing the grand attack.

'I believe it's ill,' said Louisa Mebbin, loudly in Hindustani, for the benefit of the village headman, who was in ambush in a neighbouring tree.

'Hush!' said Mrs Packletide, and at that moment the tiger commenced ambling towards his victim.

'Now, now!' urged Miss Mebbin with some excitement; 'if he doesn't touch the goat we needn't pay for it.' (The bait was an extra.)

The rifle flashed out with a loud report, and the great tawny beast sprang to one side and then rolled over in the stillness of death. In a moment a crowd of excited natives had swarmed on to the scene, and their shouting speedily carried the glad news to the village, where a thumping of tom-toms took up the chorus of

49   Production still from the film *Three Weeks* based on the novel of the same name, with Aileen Pringle, Conrad Nagel and the famous tiger skin

50   'The Tiger' by Edvard Munch. This lithograph was used to illustrate one of his most pessimistic works, 'Alpha and Omega'

51   'Tiger Devouring a Stag' by
A. L. Barye. This sculpture in
Chavrance stone was exhibited at
the *Salon*, in Paris, in 1835

52   One of a pair of Cloisonné enamel tigers whose body is imperial yellow with black stripes and feet of gilded
bronze. It dates from the Chi'ien Lung dynasty (1736-95) and belonged to the dowager Empress Tzu Hsi who used
the removable tail to indicate her mood. If the tail was stretched over the tigers back, the dowager was in a
furious temper!

53   'The Tiger Hunt' by Eugène Delacroix was painted in 1854 and was exhibited at the *Salon* the following year

54   'Tropical Storm with a Tiger' by Henri Rousseau. Painted in 1891, it was bought by the writer Georges Courteline to add to his 'museum of horrors'

55 Illustration of a tiger from *Icones Animalium,* a natural history work by Conrad Gesner dated 1560

56 'The Death of the Royal Tyger' by John Zoffany painted circa 1795. The artist is seated on the elephant to the right of the picture next to Sir John Macpherson, the man holding the gun

57   'The God Shiva, Riding a Tiger, Fighting a Demon'. Painting from Deccan,
                                                              India, eighteenth century

58   'The Triumph of Bacchus'. In this mosaic
from El Djem, Tunisia, the young god in his
chariot drawn by four tigresses is wearing a
crown of vine leaves and grapes and is
attended by Silenius. Another mosaic at
El Djem shows Bacchus with just two tigers,
his more usual source of power

60   Detail from the stock of one of Tipu Sultan's sporting guns depicting the double-headed Hindu heron being attacked by the Muslim tiger

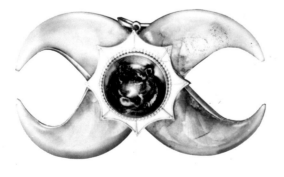

61   Victorian brooch-pendant of a painted tiger's head, set in gold, flanked by four tiger claws

62   'Tiger Shooting in India', a typical royal tiger shoot. This sketch was made during Prince Albert Victor's trip to India in 1890

63   'The Prince's First Tiger'. The Prince of Wales, later Edward VII, seated second left, showed great courage when his elephant was attacked by
the tiger

64   'Lieutenant Rice and the Tiger'. A relentless slayer of tigers, Rice is seen here saving his companion, Cornet Elliott, from a serious mauling

65   Arjan Singh crossing a river near his farm, Tiger Haven, northern India with the captive-bred tiger cub, Tara, before she took herself off to live in the wild

triumph. And their triumph and rejoicing found a ready echo in the heart of Mrs Packletide; already that luncheon-party in Curzon Street seemed immeasurably nearer.

It was Louisa Mebbin who drew attention to the fact that the goat was in death-throes from a mortal bullet-wound, while no trace of the rifle's deadly work could be found on the tiger. Evidently the wrong animal had been hit, and the beast of prey had succumbed to heart-failure, caused by the sudden report of the rifle, accelerated by senile decay. Mrs Packletide was pardonably annoyed at the discovery; but, at any rate, she was the possessor of a dead tiger, and the villagers, anxious for their thousand rupees, gladly connived at the fiction that she had shot the beast. And Miss Mebbin was a paid companion. Therefore did Mrs Packletide face the cameras with a light heart, and her pictured fame reached from the pages of the *Texas Weekly Snapshot* to the illustrated Monday supplement of the *Novoe Vremya*. As for Loona Bimberton, she refused to look at an illustrated paper for weeks, and her letter of thanks for the gift of a tiger-claw brooch was a model of repressed emotions. The luncheon-party she declined; there are limits beyond which repressed emotions become dangerous.

From Curzon Street the tiger-skin rug travelled down to the Manor House, and was duly inspected and admired by the county, and it seemed a fitting and appropriate thing when Mrs Packletide went to the County Costume Ball in the character of Diana. She refused to fall in, however, with Clovis's tempting suggestion of a primeval dance party, at which every one should wear the skins of beasts they had recently slain. 'I should be in rather a Baby Bunting condition,' confessed Clovis, 'with a miserable rabbit-skin or two to wrap up in, but then,' he added, with a rather malicious glance at Diana's proportions, 'my figure is quite as good as that Russian dancing boy's.'

'How amused everyone would be if they knew what really happened,' said Louisa Mebbin a few days after the ball.

'What do you mean?' asked Mrs Packletide quickly.

'How you shot the goat and frightened the tiger to death,' said Miss Mebbin, with her disagreeably pleasant laugh.

'No one would believe it,' said Mrs Packletide, her face changing colour as rapidly as though it were going through a book of patterns before post-time.

'Loona Bimberton would,' said Miss Mebbin. Mrs Packletide's face settled on an unbecoming shade of greenish white.

'You surely wouldn't give me away?' she asked.

'I've seen a week-end cottage near Dorking that I should rather like to buy,' said Miss Mebbin with seeming irrelevance. 'Six hundred and eighty, freehold. Quite a bargain, only I don't happen to have the money.'

Louisa Mebbin's pretty week-end cottage, christened by her 'Les Fauves', and gay in summer-time with its garden borders of tiger-lilies, is the wonder and admiration of her friends.

'It is a marvel how Louisa manages to do it,' is the general verdict.

Mrs Packletide indulges in no more big-game shooting.

'The incidental expenses are so heavy,' she confides to inquiring friends.

The largest and most impressive tiger hunts were staged by great maharajahs for the entertainment of visiting royalty (plate 62). One of the grandest tiger hunts of all time was laid on for the son of Queen Victoria, Empress of India. In these full scale hunts the guns and beaters, also mounted on elephants, would line up in a V formation. They advanced straight ahead until a tiger was spotted within the V when the flanks would close, encircling the tiger. As the ring grew smaller it was hoped that the guest of honour would be in a position to shoot the tiger. One professional hunter commented: 'if an important guest is invited to shoot he should at least see, if not shoot a tiger. To make sure he does, the kill to which the tiger returns, and the drinking holes, may be doctored with opium. Tigers can become opium addicts.'[6] On this particular hunt mounted for the Prince of Wales in 1876 certainly no opium was used (plate 63):

The tigers finding themselves hemmed in dashed furious round the circle, roaring loudly. The elephants were trumpeting, men shouting, and it was a scene of great confusion. Above all was heard the shrill voice of Sir Jung Bahadoor, hulring imprecations on the head of any who should allow the line to be broken. The ground on the side where the Prince was gradually became trampled down, but a patch was still left giving covert to the tigers. Out of this patch of ground they kept charging into the open. In one of these charges the elephant ridden by His Royal Highness was attacked. Though a staunch animal, he did not keep his front towards the tiger – but turned so as to receive the tiger upon his vast haunch. This movement sent the mahout and the other persons reeling backwards, but the Prince instantly recovered himself, coolly turned and fired.

The tiger was killed, his head being at that time very near the legs of Mr Peter Robinson, the Prince's attendant then seated behind him.[7]

At the time of the Prince's shoot the price of a trained elephant was between £200 and £400 and a further £90 was needed annually for its upkeep. Thus it was an expensive sport as a minimum of five elephants was needed to mount the most straightforward hunt. Dreadful accounts of elephants being mauled by tigers are common throughout the hundreds of volumes written on tiger hunting. Captain Mundy reported: 'no sooner had the elephant's head entered the grass, than the tigress sprang clean off the ground between his tusks, and clinging to the trunk and forehead with her claws, set to work to maul him about the jaw.'[8] The tiger was not particular where he charged, 'as the light was waining Captain P's elephant suddenly uttered a shrill scream, and came rushing out of the swamp with the tiger hanging by its teeth to the upper part of its tail.'[9] The elephants also suffered from the hunters who indiscriminately shot at their quarry regardless of the safety of their animals. The tiger on Captain P's elephant's tail 'received eight balls; when he dropped off the poor elephant's mangled tail, quite dead. The elephant survived only ten days, but it was shrewdly suspected that his more mortal wounds were inflicted by some of the sportsmen who were overzealous to rid him of his troublesome hanger on.'[10] Another accounts records how a single shot killed a tiger and an elephant as the tiger lacerated the wretched animal's head.

Not surprisingly the elephant has a deep hatred of the tiger developed over generations of maulings on hunts and in the wild, and thus shared its owners triumph at the kill: 'our elephant proclaimed his delight even more noisely than our huntsmen. The enormous beasts came to scent the carcass of their dead enemy, and turned it over with their tusks, uttering hoarse cries accompanied by a regular flourish of trumpets.'[11] An elephant will also charge a tiger: 'he rushed with the greatest fury into the thicket, and falling upon his knees, nailed the tiger with his tusks to the ground' (plate 59).[12]

The men who looked after and drove the elephants were called *mahouts*. They, too, were frequently mauled, a prime target sitting astride the elephant's neck with only the ears as protection. Sometimes they were given opium, *bhang*, to steady their nerve which, by the many accounts of injury, they needed: 'the *mahout* who had been shaken from his seat and hung onto the elephant's hind quarters, was terribly bitten and his foot crushed to pieces, but he said nothing'.[13]

Their reward for being party to such danger was to care for their elephants, whom they adored, and to have the pick of the flesh, fat and offal of the tiger.

The hunters were in comparative safety in their *howdahs*. Pads, or simple saddles, were more dangerous having no protection. Occasionally an elephant would bolt through the trees and sweep the *howdah* and the occupants off and there are many accounts of hunters plucked off pads by a determined tiger. Some were shot and wounded by their companions in the excitement of the moment.

There was an unwritten code amongst all tiger hunters that every wounded tiger must be followed up and killed. This was an exceedingly dangerous task as a wounded tiger is understandably fierce and the follow up had to be done on foot. Such was the callousness of some hunters that they would leave a wounded tiger to prey on the unarmed inhabitants of the forest or would deliberately set fire to the grass, even crops, to flush out a tiger, regardless of the villagers and their welfare. It was generally considered, after the introduction of the accurate modern rifle, that hunting from elephants was far less sporting than hunting the tiger on foot.

After World War I, tiger hunting for the European became a question of economics, the fewer tigers there were to shoot, the more expensive and exclusive the 'sport' became. Only the very rich trophy hunters or the Indian princes could stage the grand affairs with elephants and then mainly in honour of some great personage.

Despite these stories of relentless and systematic slaughter over the centuries, these 'sportsmen' only made a dent, albeit a sizeable one, in the tiger population. The near extinction of the tiger species can be attributed to its competition with man for its habitat.

10

If all the beasts were gone, man would die
Chief Seathl

'At one time in parts of India at the beginning of the last century, they [tigers] were so numerous it seemed to be a question as to whether man or the tiger would survive.'[1] Dunbar Brander was reflecting on the early 1800s when the tiger population was at its zenith. There is no possible way of knowing the exact numbers of tigers at the turn of the twentieth century but the figure generally quoted is 40,000 for India and a further 100,000 throughout the rest of Asia. By 1969 barely 5,000 tigers survived in the wild in small isolated groups.

It was then realized that if such an astounding rate of loss continued unchecked there would soon be no tigers left, other than in zoos or safari parks. Two species were already extinct, four more were listed in the I.U.C.N. *Red Data Book*, the International Union for the Conservation of Nature and Natural Resources' record of endangered species. The remaining two sub-species, the Indian and the Indo-Chinese tigers, were sinking fast.

The reasons for this rapid decline were obvious; reasons accurately pin-pointed by Captain Mundy as early as 1833 when writing of a particular tiger hunt in 1827:

> Thus in the space of about two hours, and within sight of the camp, we found and slew three tigers, a piece of good fortune rarely to be met with in these modern times, when the spread of cultivation, and the zeal of the English sportsmen have almost exterminated the breed of these animals.[2]

In addition to the growth of the human population which led to the inexorable spread of farming throughout the tiger's range and the excessive contrived slaughter, there was also a lucrative market for tiger skins.

Mundy's thoughtful attitude was unusual, for few sportsmen throughout the whole history of tiger hunting really believed that their prolific quarry could ever be shot to extinction. They occasionally expressed mild concern that they had fewer tigers to shoot than their predecessors but seldom attempted to discover the cause for this. One verbose writer sportsman in 1875 writing from Central India did comment that 'tigers are certainly now not so numerous by a great deal in many parts with which I am personally aquainted as they were even six or eight years ago'.[3]

By the turn of the century the more intelligent hunters began to exercise some measure of control in order to protect their sport. Forest reserves were divided up into hunting blocks and a closed season introduced. The Indian princes set aside vast tracts of land solely for the tiger, in order to preserve their sport. The Ranas, the former ruling family of Nepal, also kept huge tracts of Chitawan on the border with India exclusively for tiger hunting. Poaching was virtually unknown, so severe were the penalties under the new game laws. The tigers thrived as a direct result of these changes, their numbers keeping pace with those culled in the protected areas. Some areas were hunted more than others, like the central provinces of India with their many army encampments but during World War I with only a few district officers hunting, the tiger population actually increased.

Between the two world wars the relentless slaughter continued but in some of the controlled forest areas these resilient animals actually managed to increase their numbers. A report on forest administration in the United Province in 1935-6 even states that 'it is almost inevitable that as the numbers of tigers increase there will be a migration of surplus tigers into the surrounding forests'.[4]

When shooting was relaxed during World War II the tiger population expanded again. Hunting was resumed with ruthless vigour after the war. Many professional *shikar* companies sprang up to cater for the growing demand of the very rich to 'bag the ultimate of trophies'. Their clients shot with superior weapons, regardless of expense or the effect on the species and the environment. However, not all these professional *shikars* were unscrupulous. Being experts in their field, with an intimate knowledge of the tiger, a few turned conservationists once the final ban on hunting forced them out of business.

The sudden post-war demand for skins gave the poachers a new market. Everything was in their favour after independence in India.

'Villagers who had lived, in the main, within the game laws, both from fear of punishment and lack of lethal weapons, assumed that the change of authority meant freedom from control and came to consider poaching as a democratic right in a new, free society.'[5] The game laws, although still extant, were never enforced. The 'reserved' forests, formerly well managed during the British Raj, were now considered free for all. In Nepal the Ranas' tiger forests, formerly shot every few years, were heavily poached after their overthrow in 1950 as the 'people's right'. As the restrictions on owning firearms were relaxed a new type of hunter emerged. These 'cowboys' with searchlights mounted on jeeps roared through the forests blazing at anything that moved. Toxins and rodenticides, freely given by the governments to aid new agricultural schemes, were all too often used to poison tigers. Only in Bhutan, with its predominately Buddhist population that abhorred needless killing, was the tiger relatively safe in this post-war orgy.

The systematic massacre of tigers at this time was by no means confined to the Indian subcontinent. Like the British in India the French hunted the tiger for sport throughout Indo-China although not with the same ruthless dedication. The latter day political structures of Russia and China did not entirely fit with the 'elitist sport of hunting' although the many professional hunters doubtless accounted for just as many tigers as the *shikar* companies and their clients. In China there was the added incentive of the high price that was given for the carcass because of its supposed medical and mythical properties.

In Sumatra the tiger still suffers from the attentions of the oil-rich natives and expatriate staff who pursue their quarry for his skin, a prized souvenir.

The number of tigers killed for sport, self-protection or for their skin is horrendous but is in fact small compared with the effect of 'the spread of civilization' on the tiger's decline. The population of Asia increased more in the twenty-five years after World War II than in the whole century before and is now accelerating at an even faster rate. Obviously the physical boundaries of the continent cannot expand to accommodate this population explosion so it is the land within the borders that is used to feed them. Captain Mundy's comment on the spread of cultivation in 1827 was then the exception but in time it was to become the rule throughout all Asia. Hewitt describes one spot in northern India in the 1880s where a dozen tigers had been shot in a fortnight; he returned twenty-five years later to find 'the ground had been brought completely under cultivation, and no-one could have imagined that there had ever been any cover there suitable for a tiger.'[6]

In central Asia, the Caspian tiger inhabited the dense reed and *turgai* thickets in the river valleys. When the vegetation was destroyed by steppe fires or brought under cultivation for rice, tea and cotton crops and the marshes had been drained, the tiger was forced out and eventually became extinct. Parts of the Sundarbans, the aquatic home of the Royal Bengal tiger, have also been cultivated for rice, thus squeezing the tiger into smaller and smaller ranges. In China the tiger was officially declared 'an impediment to agriculture and pastoral progress' and as such was almost exterminated.

Although the drainage of swamps and the use of former unproductive land for farming whittled away the tiger's range, it was the destruction of the forests and jungles that most affected the tiger. The enormous demand for timber during the last war began the indiscriminate felling of the mature hardwood forests of Asia. Unfortunately this trend, a valuable foreign currency earner, has continued and escalated to the present-day level. The cleared forests are either taken for agriculture or planted with unsuitable softwoods. With these new plantations there is no undergrowth, and like the cultivated areas, they cannot 'hold' a tiger. With no cover there can be no tigers. In Nepal the malaria-carrying mosquito effectively kept man from cultivating the former Rana-controlled forests of the Chitawan Valley. A United States aid project checked the spread of these mosquitoes, so encouraging the colonization of parts of that 1,000 square mile bastion of tiger country, an all too common example of man moving in at the expense of the tiger.

In the coastal mountain ranges of China the unending search for firewood has effectively destroyed the forests. Full-scale commercial ventures that felled the forests of Sumatra and Java have critically reduced the tiger's habitat, forcing these vulnerable sub-species into smaller and less suitable areas. In Malaya the tiger fares rather better than elsewhere because in that country there has been less damage to his habitat. Little is known of the forestry operations in war-torn Vietnam, Laos and Democratic Kampuchea, but the news is unlikely to be encouraging as the tiger has probably been much disturbed by man. In parts of Vietnam millions of hectares of forest were defoliated by the United States Air Force using napalm and arsenic-based chemicals. The resurgence of secondary growth created ideal conditions for the tiger and his prey species but much of the area was heavily mined and 'booby-trapped' and is littered with unexploded shells and bombs. Although these obstacles now effectively keep the areas free of humans and leave the tiger in peace, he, too, can be blown up by accident.

The fate of the tiger is not only affected by hunting and the loss of habitat to forestry and cultivation. The ever-expanding Asian population requires more and more space in which to live. Over the last few decades even the remotest areas have been opened up for settlement. These developments disturb the formerly wild areas, hounding the few remaining tigers and their prey species to extinction. The tiger has to contend with major hydro-electric power stations, oil refineries and oil fields, all with their operators, motor-trucks and helipads.

In the conflict between man and the tiger it is invariably man that wins. The conflict is entirely of man's making, for the tiger has no quarrel with humans. In India there are now an estimated 300 million cattle. A very large percentage of these give neither milk, food nor leather and are prevented from being slaughtered, even for humane reasons, on religious grounds. These cattle either stray or are driven into the feeding grounds of the tiger's prey species, competing for their food and spreading disease. The prey species are effectively driven off leaving the tiger no choice but to take these cattle to survive. In many cases a villager will cultivate right up to the boundary of the tiger's range. There have been reports of a tigress giving birth to her cubs actually in a sugar cane field. Very occasionally a cane cutter has been mauled or sometimes killed by a mother protecting her cubs. Farmers have been killed or attacked in their paddy fields for the same reasons, and still the tiger is labelled a man-eater.

It is a short-sighted farmer who complains that his weak and near worthless cattle are being 'lifted' by a tiger. The farmer struggles to grow enough food for his family, guarding it night and day against wild pig, deer and destructive monkeys. If the tiger takes domestic cattle he is, in fact, doing the farmer a service for his very presence will keep those herbivores off the farmer's crops. The value of cattle taken rarely exceeds his value as a 'game keeper'. In his capacity of controller, the tiger's worth has always been appreciated by some like this *Jagheerdar* (headman of an Indian village) described by a nineteenth-century forester:

While sitting at breakfast we were alarmed by hearing cries of distress proceeding from the Jagheerdar's hut, and on running out to ascertain the cause, we found old Kumah in a furious state of excitement, his left hand firmly fixed in the woolly pate of the hopeful scion of the house, and belabouring him soundly with a stout bamboo. We inquired what crime young Mohadeen had been guilty of to bring upon himself such a storm of parental indignation, and learned to our astonishment that it was owing to his having killed a tiger. To most this feat would have been considered brave in a boy of fifteen but not so the old man who recognized the value of the tiger to the village. [7]

This perceptive headman recognized one of the important functions of the tiger. As one of the great carnivores the tiger stands at the pinnacle of the wild life pyramid, a primary predator who controls stocks of prey species, that in turn affect the environment. If man in his ignorance lops off the pinnacle, then a fearful chain reaction starts that alters the structure of the pyramid, making it unstable.

An illustration of this occurred in the Red Indian reserve of Kiabab in the United States of America. Congress passed a preservation order on a particularly rare species of deer only to be found in the Kiabab, but did not put a preservation order on the mountain lion as it was considered dangerous vermin. Eventually the lion was hunted to extinction for sport and for the high price its pelt fetched. The controlling factor removed, the deer multiplied unchecked. They began to strip the bark of the aspen, the predominant tree, as they were short of scrub and grass on which to browse. The young saplings were also eaten leaving nothing to replace the dead and decaying trees. The cool of a forest condenses the vapour of the air which in turn falls as rain, and so, with fewer trees, it rained less, and the water table fell. With no rain the undergrowth shrivelled up and the Red Indians in the reserve suffered from crop failure and lack of pasture for their stock and horses. They in turn began to die out. Those that survived moved from the barren land believing that a curse from heaven had driven them away.

The devastating effects of interfering with the environment can be seen in the desert near Kahtan, in the Takla Makan region in the far west of China, which was once 'tiger country'. A Swedish archaeologist discovered that the city there had been constructed almost entirely of wood, undoubtedly felled from the surrounding forest. With the loss of the forest and the proximity of man the tiger moved away. What remained of the forest and the cultivations around the city soon dwindled and, with no rainfall, erosion set in and reduced the environs to desert.

A similar example in the last fifty years is the town of Gorakhpur in the United Province of India. In the 1930s the town 'for a long time had to be protected against the ravages of tigers by lines of fires'. [8] Today there is not a tiger to be seen near this straggling city set in a barren sun-baked wilderness.

Those who advocate that the tiger is better off in a zoo or safari park living a trouble-free existence clearly do not appreciate the ecosystems of nature or the habits of the tiger. Some of these people believe the tiger is better protected in captivity, where they breed with relative ease, in quite large numbers and more frequently than in the wild. Others believe that nature is cruel. Nature is not cruel. Animals are not ruled by fear as Rudyard Kipling suggests in his *Second Jungle Book*, but by hunger or thirst. Where permitted by man, tigers live carefree lives – except where experience has taught caution.

For the most part these latter day Polito Menagerie owners are quick to defend the presence of tigers in their zoos and safari parks as their bid to save an endangered species from extinction, but it is likely their real motive is financial. There are of course many notable exceptions among these establishments where scientific study is stressed and regular cross breeding occurs with the establishment of sperm banks. London, Basle, Frankfurt, Phoenix, San Diego and Delhi zoos are among the pioneers of this work.

Although adequately fed and watered, a caged tiger can never be happy, even if he has been bred in captivity. Six paces at the most in each direction on a concrete floor and behind iron bars is no substitute for the many miles a tiger normally travels in a night when hunting in the wild. Swimming, another favourite pastime of the tiger, is nearly always denied him. Without these and the other necessities, it is no wonder that tigers become lethargic and deteriorate. The normally acute eyesight, hearing and sense of smell fade from lack of use. These defects become increasingly pronounced with in-breeding. The result from the average zoo is a tiger which is a mere caricature of his former majestic self.

The now fashionable safari parks are marginally better than the average zoo but still open parkland is no substitute for a home range of forest or jungle with cover, game and water. As with the zoos, there are exceptions, like the Marwell Zoological Park near Winchester, Hampshire. Here the accent is on gathering practical knowledge that can be applied to conservation in the field and on educating the public rather than concentrating on the gate receipts – although these too are important to finance the projects.

Private collectors like John Aspinall, make a significant contribution to the greater understanding of many of the endangered species. John Aspinall's breeding programme of Indian and Siberian tigers has been particularly helpful. His 'zoo parks' at Howletts and Port Lympne, both in Kent, are open to the public most of the year.

For a tigress to teach the basic skills of stalking and hunting to her cubs can take up to two years of intensive tuition. A tiger cub bred in a zoo or safari park cannot possibly be taught these essential skills by his captive-bred parent and so would be helpless if returned to his natural habitat. However, 'Billy' Arjan Singh, a great naturalist and conservationist, has achieved what was thought to be impossible by returning a captive-bred tigress to the wild. In a scheme sponsored by Frankfurt Zoo a tigress cub, Tara, from Twycross Zoo was sent to Tiger Haven, Arjan Singh's farm in the Dudhwa National Park on the Indian-Nepalese border. There she roamed completely free and every day accompanied Arjan Singh on his rounds in the forest (plate 65). Gradually she began making sorties to the forest on her own, becoming increasingly independent. Eventually she left 'home' completely when her mating call was answered by a tiger. She has been seen again, once, remarkably, being taught to hunt by the tiger. The success of the operation was in doubt for some time when she disappeared, but Tara has recently been photographed, proving that a captive-bred tiger can be returned successfully to the wild. It is encouraging to think that this reintroduction could work on a larger scale, but only when the nations concerned are ready to receive and protect them for ever. For some sub-species it is already too late.

The extensive search and subsequent photographic evidence of Tara was sponsored by a new organization, the International Trust for Nature Conservation. This trust is made up of a team of dedicated conservationists who channel all their funds, expertise and energies into a few selected projects, like the tiger and leopard schemes at Tiger Haven. One of the principal advantages of the I.T.N.C. is that their sponsors can actually see where their money is being spent and are kept fully informed of particular projects.

Unquestionably the tiger's only place is in his natural habitat, free from the interference of man. It is still a close run race between the tiger's survival and his destruction. In some countries the race has already been lost, in others the tiger is disappearing fast while elsewhere there are encouraging signs that the tiger population is on the increase.

The last recorded small Bali tigress was shot in 1937. Reports that a few survived in the west of the island were unfounded. Since a Caspian tiger was shot in Iran in 1957 there have been a few hopeful signs of pug marks, like those in the Elburtz mountains, and sightings in eastern Turkey, but these have not been repeated so there is little hope that any of this species survives.

There are tragically few Javan tigers left in Java. In the latest survey, 1978, evidence rather than sightings of only three, possibly five, tigers was found. With only one captive-bred tigress in Budapest Zoo it is all too likely that this species will soon become extinct, a far cry from the 1830s 'when the Javan tiger was found all over the island'.[9]

Numerically the Sumatran tiger is stronger than the Javan. A conservative estimate puts their numbers at 800, scattered over the island in small groups. Although there are still viable breeding stocks, hunters and the loss of environment are steadily whittling away the numbers.

A report from *Novostrov*, the Russian press agency, in 1979 confirms that, despite belated conservation measures, there are no Caspian tigers left in their last known habitat in the U.S.S.R., a spot called Tiger Gulch in Tagikistan. The same press release announced that 'naturalists believe that there is no longer any danger of the Amur or Ussuri [Siberian] tiger dying out in the Soviet far east. Thanks to strict protection their number has doubled to about 200 in the last 20 years'. Conflicting reports have come out of the People's Republic of China on the numbers of Siberian tigers still extant there and in Korea. Some believe that there are as many as 100 or 200 in the northernmost Heilungkiang Province but a 1973 report suggests, regrettably, that only 'several tens of tigers remain in China and Korea'.[10]

Although the numbers of Siberian tigers in China are minimal, the Chinese tiger population is even smaller. In a survey in 1978 this tiger slipped from being 'very rare' to 'on the verge of extinction'.[11] A few tigers exist in isolated pockets about the Yangtse river valley where they compete with the Chinese for land. The latest news is that the decline has been checked but this has not been authenticated.

The little that is known about the numbers of the Indo-Chinese tiger indicates that he is faring better than the other sub-species. The population is not large being in the 'very low thousands' and is still on the decline. It may be some time before any information on numbers comes out of those war-torn countries of south-east Asia where it would appear that the preservation of the tiger is not a high priority. Despite having the best tiger forests, the number of Indo-Chinese tigers in Malaysia is falling from an estimated 3,000 in 1954 to between 600 and 700 in 1978, and is still declining. The tiger's lot is little different in Thailand where the population of 500 is also on the decline. The census carried out in 1960 showed 1,125 tigers to the east of the Irrawaddy, the great Burmese river that divides the two species of tiger, the Indo-Chinese and the Indian. Since that date the Burmese borders have been closed to foreigners but the news of the tiger population is disturbing as the species is believed to be 'much depleted although widely if thinly scattered and to have completely disappeared from many of its old haunts such as the Maymyo Game Sanctuary'.[12]

Across the Irrawaddy the same 1960 census revealed 496 Indian tigers, but they too were sharing the same fate as the Indo-Chinese tigers. Towards the end of the 1960s the fact that the race type of the species, the Indian tiger, was rapidly heading towards extinction was finally appreciated. For decades naturalists, like the celebrated E.P. Gee and the ex-hunter Jim Corbett, had been canvassing the plight of the tiger and the reasons for his decline, but such was the power of the *shikar* lobby and the short-sightedness of the government that their warnings went unheeded. However, the position was eventually understood in 1969 when the total number was thought to have fallen to only 2,500 in India. Bangladesh was thought to support a further 150, Nepal about the same, Bhutan 200 and Burma not many more. The total, a possible 3,500, was a far cry from the estimated 40,000 at the turn of the century and the figure of 30,000 at the beginning of World War II. These figures were presented to the I.U.C.N. Congress in New Delhi which resulted in a resolution to add the Indian tiger to the I.U.N.C. *Red Data Book* which lists endangered species.

Once the tiger's plight had been registered an all-out ban on hunting was passed by the governments of all countries in the Indian tiger's range. The export of skins was also prohibited. The battle for this legislation was hard fought but proved even harder to put into operation. The hunting ban was openly flaunted, often by those with the authority to enforce it, the excuse being that every tiger killed was a proven man-eater. The penalties for killing tigers were small when compared with the inflated prices of tiger skins the export ban produced. Even today skins can be bought openly in the New Market in Calcutta. Clearly legislation by itself was not enough to check the dwindling stock of tigers. In order to act effectively, the exact tiger population and its various locations had to be established. In 1972 a census, carried out by nearly 5,000 men in two massive swoops, showed an estimated 1,827 tigers in the whole of India. Armed with this information, Guy Mountfort, a founder member of the World Wildlife Fund, prepared a paper for the Fund outlining his proposals for saving the tiger. After some initial opposition, mainly financial, and the uncertainty of its reception in the countries concerned, the scheme 'Operation Tiger' was adopted. Finance for the project came quickly by way of a world-wide appeal that raised, not the target figure of 1 million dollars but 1.7 million dollars. The money came from donations and the sale of books, pictures and almost anything with a tiger logo. David Shepherd's brilliant picture 'Tiger Fire' raised £120,000 in signed lithographs. The success of the scheme showed the world cared about the tiger.

The suspected opposition to 'Project Tiger', the Indian version of

'Operation Tiger', did not materialize. The way having been carefully paved by Guy Mountfort, Mrs Indira Gandhi took up the scheme with enthusiasm and appointed a cabinet minister, Dr Karem Singh, as chairman and Kailash Sankhala, director of the Delhi Zoological Park, as overseer of the six year plan. Two million pounds, a massive sum considering India's economic and social problems at that time, was voted to the scheme. It set a fine example to the rest of Asia.

The aim of 'Project Tiger' is to protect specific areas by eliminating the interference of man and letting nature take its course. This interference covers everything from forestry operations, the grazing of domestic stock and poaching to the removal of whole villages.

Since 'Project Tiger' was launched on 1 April 1973 eleven reserves have been established, each in a separate state and containing different types of tiger habitat. The eleven are situated in Bandipur, (Karnataka), Corbett (Uttar Pradesh), Kanha (Madhya Pradesh), Manas (Assam), Melghat (Maharashtra),Palamau (Bihar), Periyar (Kerala), Ranthambhor and Sariska (Rajasthan), Simlipal Orrisa and Sundarbans (West Bengal). There are also 125 smaller sanctuaries throughout India, perhaps the best known being 'Billy' Arjan Singh's 'Tiger Haven' on the border with Nepal.

Mountfort went to Bangladesh, which was then only just recovering from a devastating war, and persuaded the government to set aside part of the Sundarbans as a tiger reserve. Together with the Indian reserve in the Sundarbans, the two form one of the largest natural wild life parks in the continent.

Proof of the success of the scheme is beginning to show. There is a marked increase in the number of tigers in each of the reserves and this trend is encouraging. Despite this magnificent start, continued success is by no means assured. Tigers are resilient animals and given the right facilities, notably protection, they will increase up to, but not beyond, their optimum number for each reserve. But even in some of these reserves the tiger is still disturbed. Villagers still graze their cattle in the tigers' forests, the felling of hardwood continues, possibly to offset the loss of revenue from the 12,000 square kilometres given over to the tiger.

In Nepal the conservation of the tiger is centred on the Royal Chitawan National Park, the 1,000 square mile valley between the Siwalicks and the Himalayas, with another two reserves, Karnali and Sukla Phanta, to the far west of the country. Coinciding with the ban on hunting, the Nepalese Government adopted the World Wildlife Fund's proposals in 'Operation Tiger' and designated 210 square miles of the Royal Chitawan National Park as a sanctuary for

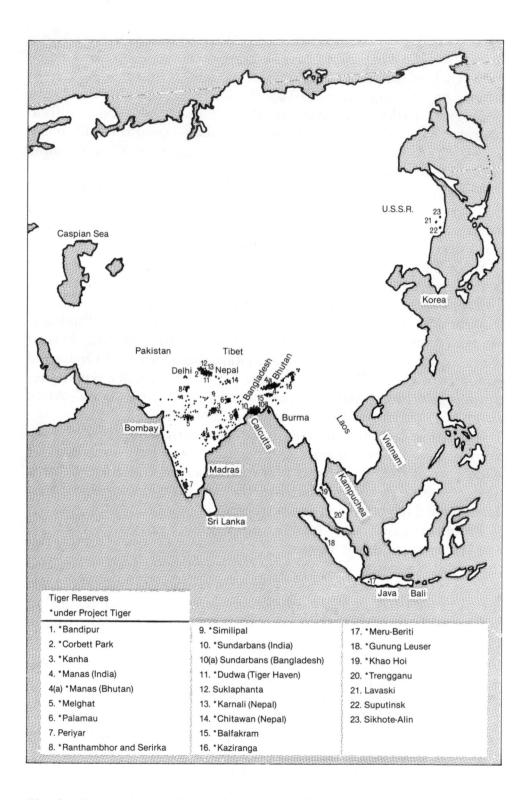

Fig. 9   Reserves throughout the tiger's world range

the preservation of tigers. Adjacent to this reserve is an hotel, Tiger Tops, where wildlife enthusiasts can stay and watch the fauna of the reserve in its natural state. The thorough studies and intimate knowledge of this Reserve's tigers since 1972, have made the Tiger Tops director of wildlife activities, Dr Charles McDougal, one of the leading authorities on tigers today.

The retort of high powered rifles still echoes round the *terai* forests of the Royal Chitawan National Park. Armed men still ride on elephants at the head of a funnel of beaters as they draw a known tiger range. There are still cries of 'Hey, Hey, *bagh, bagh,* tiger, tiger!' as the flash of orange and black and white streaks through the trees. As the tiger approaches the guns a single shot is fired. The tiger, hit in the flank, continues crashing through the undergrowth. The beaters follow to claim their prize. But these are no Rana hunters, or even poachers, but Nepalese and American scientists sponsored by the Smithsonian Institute in Washington and the American arm of the World Wildlife Fund. The tiger is not dead, merely heavily sedated by a tranquillizer dart.

It was no accident that the Smithsonian chose the Chitawan Valley to study the tiger for the Nepalese government take their conservation seriously – the army patrol the reserve day and night and take a fatalistic view of poaching. The scientists spent five years in a management-orientated, scientific study of the tiger in the wild. Their method of monitoring their tigers was simple. Twenty-six tigers, mostly sub-adults, were selected, tranquillized and fitted with a light radio transmitter built into a collar fitted round their necks. From then on their movements were followed, either by receivers on the ground or from light aircraft. These movements were plotted, giving the scientists an accurate picture of the tiger's life in the day time, their kills, feeding patterns, associations with other tigers and matings and, most significantly, their search for new home ranges once the family group had split up. The study proved to be a success and their findings of great practical use. The original reserve has now been increased to 360 square miles with the aid of a fund set up by the Frankfurt Zoological Society which will allow the increasing tiger population to expand into new home ranges. Eleven tigers are still collared and their movements monitored, not only by radio tracking but also by traditional methods. For obvious reasons the radio tracking is useless at night and as the tiger is a nocturnal animal there is still much to be learned about his night time habits. The results of these exhaustive studies and the continuing work in the field have done much to further the understanding of the tiger and his habitat.

These conservation measures were not confined to saving the Indian tiger. Other countries were actively involved in their own projects to save their particular sub-species. Tiger hunting and the export of skins was universally banned, with the exception of Burma where, according to a local newspaper article, 'hunting and dealing in tiger skins were so lucrative that buying centres have been opened in Akyab and Momeik'. [13]

With the expertise and financial backing of 'Project Tiger' the Indonesian government set up the Meru-Beriti Game Reserve in 1972 to protect the pathetically few remaining Javan tigers. In Sumatra, where despite legislation tigers are shot and skins exported, the government has set aside nearly one million hectares at the Gunung Leuser Reserve for the tiger and the many other threatened species. So far the scheme is proving a success, but the tiger is so persecuted in other parts of the island that the overall position is still not healthy.

The Indo-Chinese tiger is being protected by the Malayan government in a reserve being set up in the state of Trengganu as part of a five year plan. In Thailand there are already four reserves, the National Park at Khao Noi and three sanctuaries in the upper basin of the Khwae Noi river system. The day may still come when the governments of the war-torn Vietnam, Laos and Democratic Kampuchea view the tiger in his proper light and consider him worth saving.

Although they were too late to save the Caspian tiger, the Russians have had some success with their conservation programme for the Siberian tiger. That sub-species has doubled and is still increasing in their Sikhote Alin Reserve of 310,000 hectares, the Suputinsk Reserve of 16,500 hectares and the Lavaski Reserve where a policy of *laissez faire* has produced encouraging results.

A start has been made on planning a tiger reserve in China. With the increasing political and cultural ties between China and the West the tiger's chance of survival may be increased.

In some areas these conservation programmes may have come too late, for not all these reserves hold an equal chance of success. The I.U.N.C. Survival Service Commission states that an animal like the tiger needs a contiguous population of at least 300 to maintain a viable gene pool. All known populations of tigers are below this figure with little chance of natural genetic exchanges with other groups.

The future of the tiger depends entirely upon man. A fine start has been made among those who believe in saving the tiger for future generations. The results of 'Project Tiger' are encouraging but will count for little unless man is willing to share his environment with his fellow creatures. Since the earliest civilizations, the tiger has been a symbol to mankind, representing power and strength, good and evil, courage and ferocity, sometimes even luck. It would be a tragedy if this most beautiful and free of animals was lost to the world forever. The tiger's survival lies in all our hands.

References

Chapter 3

1 P. Hanley, *Tiger Trails in Assam*
2 A. Strachan, *Mauled by a Tiger*
3 F. C. Hicks, *Forty Years among the Wild Animals of India*
4 R. I. Pocock, 'A Lion Tiger Hybrid', article in *The Field*, February 1929

Chapter 4

1 H. Shakespear, *Wild Sports in India*
2 William Blake, 'The Tiger' from *The New Oxford Book of English Verse*
3 Richard Perry, *The World of the Tiger*
4 Philip Trench, *Tiger Hunting, A Day's Sport in the East*
5 Captain T. Williamson, *Oriental Field Sports*
6 *Ibid.*
7 Edward Ives, *A Voyage from India to England*

Chapter 5

1 Lockwood Kipling, *Beast and Man in India*
2 L. A. Cammiade, 'Man-Eaters and Were-Tigers', article in *Man*, October 1931
3 Asutash Bhattacharyya, 'The Tiger Cult and its Literature in Lower Bengal', article in *Man in India,* Vol. XXVII, 1947
4 *Ibid.*
5 Chalmers Werner, *A Dictionary of Chinese Mythology*
6 William Edmunds, *Pointers and Clues to Chinese and Japanese Art*
7 T. Volker, *The Animal in Far Eastern Art*
8 Aesop, *Aesop's Fables*

Chapter 6

1 Caius Plinius Secundus, *Naturalis Historiæ*
2 *Ibid.*
3 John Guillim, *Display of Heraldrie*
4 John Evelyn taken from Wilfred Blunt, *The Ark in the Park*
5 I.U.C.N., *The Red Data Book*
6 H. Shakespear, *Wild Sports in India*
7 J. Forsyth, *Highlands of Central India*
8 A. Beatson, *A View of the Origin and Conduct of the War with Tippoo Sultann*
9 Major M. Wilkes, *Historical Sketches of South India*
10 P. Meadows Taylor, *Tippoo Sultaun*
11 Letter in *The Gentleman's Magazine*, July 1793
12 Dr Mildred Archer, *Tippoo's Tiger*
13 Edited by E. Gurwood, *The Dispatches of Field Marshal, The Duke of Wellington,* postscript to a letter to General Harris from Arthur Wellesley, 5 May 1799, taken from D. Forrest, *The Tiger of Mysore*
14 D. Forrest, *The Tiger of Mysore*
15 J. Forbes, *Oriental Memoirs*

Chapter 7

1 Basil Taylor, *Stubbs*
2 *Ibid.*
3 Thomas Bewick, *A General History of Quadrupeds*
4 C. R. Leslie, *Autobiographical Recollections* taken from Wilfred Blunt, *The Ark in the Park*
5 Her Majesty Queen Victoria's Journal entry for 23 February 1839, taken from *Animal Painting*, the catalogue for the exhibition held at the Queen's Gallery, Buckingham Palace, London, 1966-7
6 *Ibid.* Journal entry 29 January 1839
7 James MacKay, *The Animaliers*
8 Guisseppe Marchione, *Delacroix*
9 James MacKay, *The Animaliers*
10 *Ibid.*
11 *Ibid.*
12 Werner Timm, *The Graphic Art of Edvard Munch*
13 William Blake, 'The Tiger', from *The New Oxford Book of English Verse*

Chapter 8

1 From 1585 prayer book, cited in compact edition of *Oxford English Dictionary*
2 Satir, *Poems Reform*, Poem XIV, cited in compact edition of *Oxford English Dictionary*
3 Geoffrey Chaucer, *The Canterbury Tales*, cited in Beryl Roland, *Animals with Human Faces*
4 William Shakespeare, *The Third Part of King Henry the Sixth*, Act One, Scene IV
5 William Shakespeare, *King Henry the Fifth*, Act Three, Scene I
6 *Daily Inter Ocean*, Chicago, 14 February 1888
7 R. P. Knight, *An Account of the Remains of the Worship of Priapus*
8 Martial, *The Epigrams*, Book VIII, No. 26, cited in R. G. Burton, *The Book of the Tiger*
9 Anon.
10 Rudyard Kipling, *The Jungle Book*
11 Elinor Glyn, *Three Weeks*
12 Anon.
13 Elizabeth Veale, *The English Fur Trade in the Latter Middle Ages*

Chapter 9

1 From a letter reproduced in James Forbes, *Oriental Memoirs*
2 Colonel W. Rice, *Tiger Shooting in India*
3 Colonel W. Rice, *Indian Game*
4 Philip Trench, *Tiger Hunting, A Day's Sport in the East*
5 Saki, (H. H. Monro) *Short Stories*
6 Jon and Rumer Godden, *Shivas Pigeons, An Experience in India*
7 Shikare and Tomasha, *The Prince of Wales in India*
8 Captain A. Mundy, *Pen and Pencil Sketches being the Journal of a Tour of India*
9 *Ibid.*
10 *Ibid.*
11 *Ibid.*
12 *Ibid.*
13 *Ibid.*

Chapter 10

1 A. Dunbar Brander, *Wild Animals in Central India*
2 Captain A. Mundy, *Pen and Pencil Sketches being the Journal of a Tour of India*
3 J. Forsyth, *Highlands of Central India*
4 C. McDougal, *The Face of the Tiger*
5 Richard Perry, *The World of the Tiger*

6 J. Hewitt, *Jungle Trails in Northern India*
7 W. Campbell, *The Old Forest Ranger*
8 J. Hewitt, *Jungle Trails in Northern India*
9 I.U.C.N., *The Red Data Book*
10 *Ibid.*
11 *Ibid.*
12 *Ibid.*
13 *Ibid.*

Bibliography

Books

ADAMS, ARTHUR   *Travels in Japan and Manchuria*

AESOP   *Aesop's Fables,* Translation by S. Croxall, Longmans, London, 1818

ALEXANDER, PETER (Ed.) *Shakespeare, The Complete Works,* Collins, 1951

ALLEN, G. M.   *Mammals of China and Mongolia,* American Museum of Natural History, New York, 1938

ANDERSON, MARY   *The Medieval Carver,* Cambridge University Press, 1938
Animal Carvings in British Churches, Cambridge University Press, 1938

ARCHER, DR MILDRED   *Tippoo's Tiger,* H.M.S.O., London, 1959

ASH, BRIAN   *Tiger in Your Tank,* Cassells, London, 1969

ASPINALL, JOHN   *The Best of Friends,* Macmillan, London, 1976

BALL, KATHERINE   *Decorative Motives of Oriental Art,* The Bodley Head, London, 1927

BANDINELLI, R. BIANCHI   *Roman Art to A.D. 200,* Thames and Hudson, London, 1970

BANNERMAN, HELEN   *The Story of Little Black Sambo,* Grant Richards, London, 1899

BAZÉ, WILLIAM — *Tiger, Tiger*, Elek Books, London, 1957

BEATSON, A. — *A View of the Origin and Conduct of the War with Tippoo Sultann*, Nicol, London, 1800

BENNETT, E. T. — *The Tower Menagerie*, Robert Jennings, London, 1829

BEWICK, THOMAS — *A General History of Quadrupeds*, Hodgson, Beilby and Bewick, Newcastle-upon-Tyne, 1790

BLOUNT, MARGARET — *Animal Lands*, Hutchinson, London, 1974

BLUNT, WILFRED — *The Ark in the Park, the Zoo in the Nineteenth Century*, Hamish Hamilton, London, 1976

BRANDER, A. DUNBAR — *Wild Animals in Central India*, E Arnold London, 1923

BURTON, R. G. — *The Book of the Tiger*, Hutchinson, London, 1933
The Tiger Hunters, Hutchinson, London, 1936
Wellington's Campaign in India, Superintendent Government Printing, Calcutta, 1908

CAMPBELL, W. — *The Old Forest Ranger*, How and Parsons, London, 1842

CHAMPION, F. W. — *With Camera in Tigerland*, Chatto and Windus, London, 1927
The Jungle in Sunlight and Shadow, Chatto and Windus, London, 1933

CLARK, KENNETH — *Animals and Men*, Thames and Hudson, London, 1977

COPENHAGEN, NY CARLSBERG — *Tillag Til*, Ny Carlsberg, Copenhagen, 1951

CORBETT, J. — *Man Eaters of Kumaon*, Oxford University Press, London, 1944
The Temple Tiger, Oxford University Press, London, 1952

CUNNINGHAM, ALLAN — *Lives of the most Eminent British Painters*, John Murray, London, 1823

EARDLY-WILMOT, Sir S.   *Forest Life and Sport in India,* Edward
Arnold, London, 1910
*The Life of the Tiger and the
Elephant,* Edward Arnold,
London, 1933

EDMUNDS, WILLIAM H.   *Pointers and Clues to Chinese and Japanese
Art,* Sampson Low Marston, London,
1934, reprint 1974

ELLISON, BERNARD   *The Prince of Wales in India,* Heinemann,
London, 1925

FAYER, Sir JOSEPH   *The Royal Tiger of Bengal,* J. and
A. Churchill, London, 1875
*Notes on the Visit of their Royal Highnesses
the Prince of Wales and the Duke of
Edinburgh to India, 1870, 75 and 76,*
Kirby and Endean, London, 1879

FORBES, JAMES   *Oriental Memoirs,* 3 vols., R. Bentley,
London, 1834-5

FORREST, DENYS   *The Tiger of Mysore, the Life and Death of
Tipu Sultan,* Chatto and Windus,
London, 1970

FORSYTH, J.   *Highlands of Central India,* Chapman and
Hall, London, 1919

FOX-DAVIES, A. C.   *A Complete Guide to Heraldry,* Nelson,
London, 1909, revised by J. P. Brooke-
Little, 1969

FRADIER, GEORGES   *Mosaiques de Tunisie El Djem,* Edition
Ceres, Tunis, 1976

GARDNER, HELEN (Ed.)   *The New Oxford Book of English Verse,*
Oxford University Press, Oxford, 1972

GEE, E. P.   *The Wild Life of India,* Collins, London,
1964

GESTNER, CONRAD   *Icones Animalium,* London, 1560

GILBY, Sir WALTER   *The Life of Stubbs,* Vinton and Co,
London, 1898

GLYN, ELINOR   *Three Weeks,* Duckworth, London, 1954

GODDEN, JON   *Shivas Pigeons, an Experience in India,*
  and RUMER   Chatto and Windus, 1972

GREENWOOD, JAMES   *Wild Sports of the World,* S. O. Beeton,
London, 1862

GUILLIM, JOHN   *Display of Heraldrie,* R. and J. Bonwicke,
London, 1724

HANLEY, P. — *Tiger Trails in Assam*, Robert Hale, London, 1961

HARRIS, H. A. — *Sport in Ancient Greece and Rome*, Thames and Hudson, London, 1972

HAVELOCK, C. M. — *Hellenistic Art*, Phaidon, London, 1961

HEWITT, J. — *Jungle Trails in Northern India*, Methuen, London, 1938

HICKS, F. C. — *Forty Years among the Wild Animals of India*, Pioneer Press, Allahabad, 1910

I.U.C.N. — *The Red Data Book*, Geneva, 1978

IVES, EDWARD — *A Voyage from England to India in the Year MD CC LIV*, Edward and Charles Dilly, London, 1773

KEAY, CAROLYN — *Henri Rousseau*, Academy Editions, London, 1976

KIPLING, LOCKWOOD — *Beast and Man in India*, Macmillan, London, 1891

KIPLING, RUDYARD — *The Jungle Book*, Macmillan, London, 1899

KNIGHT, RICHARD PAYNE — *An Account of the Remains of the Worship of Priapus*, T. Spilsbury, London, 1786

LARKIN, DAVID — *Rousseau*, Ballantine Books, New York, 1975

LINKS, J. G. — *The Book of Fur*, James Barrie, London, 1976

McDOUGAL, CHARLES — *The Face of the Tiger*, Rivington/André Deutsch, London, 1977

MACKAY, JAMES A. — *The Animaliers*, Ward Lock, London, 1973

MARCHIONE, GUISSEPPE — *Delacroix*, Dolphin Art Books, London, 1969

MOUNTFORT, GUY — *Back from the Brink*, Hutchinson, London, 1978

Tigers, David and Charles, Newton Abbott, 1973

MUNDY, CAPTAIN A. — *Pen and Pencil Sketches being the Journal of a Tour of India*, John Murray, London, 1833

NASH, E. — *Pictorial Dictionary of Ancient Rome*, Deutches Archaeologisches Institut, Rome, 1961

NATIONAL PORTRAIT GALLERY — *Exhibition Catalogue of John Zoffany Exhibition*, London, 1974

PERRY, RICHARD — *The World of the Tiger*, Cassells, London, 1974

PLINIUS SECUNDUS, CAIUS — *Naturalis Historiæ*, translated by H. Rackham, Heinemann, London, 1967

RICE, COLONEL W. — *Tiger Shooting in India*, W. H. Allen, London, 1857
Indian Game, W. H. Allen, London, 1859

ROLAND, BERYL — *Animals with Human Faces*, University of Tennessee Press, Knoxville, 1973

ROSTOVTZEV, MICHAEL I. — *The Animal Style in South Russia and China*, Princeton Monographs, Princeton, 1929

SAKI (H. H. MUNRO) — *Short Stories*, The Bodley Head, London, 1963

SANKHALA, KAILASH — *Tigerland*, Collins, London, 1975
Tiger!, Collins, London, 1977

SCHALLER, G. B. — *The Deer and the Tiger*, University of Chicago Press, Chicago, 1969

SEN, ASSIS — *Animal Motifs in Ancient Indian Art* Mukhopadhyay, Calcutta, 1972

SHAKESPEAR, H. — *Wild Sports in India*, Smith and Elder London, 1860

SHIKARE and TOMASHA — *The Prince of Wales in India, The Winter Tour of 1875-6*, Dent, London, 1876

SINGH, ARJAN — *Tiger Haven*, Macmillan, London, 1973

STRACHAN, A. — *Mauled by a Tiger*, Murray Press, Edinburgh, 1933

TAYLOR, BASIL — *Stubbs*, Phaidon, London, 1971

TAYLOR, P. MEADOWS — *Tippoo Sultaun, A Tale of the Mysore War*, C. Keegan Paul, London, 1880

TIMM, WERNER — *The Graphic Art of Edvard Munch*, Studio Vista, London, 1969

TOYNBEE, JOCELYN — *Animals in Roman Life and Art*, Thames and Hudson, London, 1976

TRENCH, PHILIP — *Tiger Hunting, A Day's Sport in the East*, Hodgson and Graves, London, 1836

VEALE, ELIZABETH M. — *The English Fur Trade in the Latter Middle Ages*, Oxford University Press, London, 1966

VOLKER, T.	*The Animal in Far Eastern Art*, E. J. Brill, Leiden, 1975
WERNER, CHALMERS	*A Dictionary of Chinese Mythology*, Kelly and Walsh, Shanghai, 1932
WHITE, T. H.	*Book of Beasts*, Jonathan Cape, London, 1954
WILKES, MAJOR M.	*Historical Sketches of South India, in an Attempt to trace the History of Mysore*, 3 vols., Lowe, London, 1810
WILLIAMS, C. A. S.	*Outlines of Chinese Symbolism and Art Motives*, Customs College Press, Peking, 1931
WILLIAMSON, CAPTAIN T.	*Oriental Field Sports*, Orme, London, 1807
WORLD WILDLIFE FUND	*Year Book*, Geneva, 1978-79

Magazines

The Daily Inter Ocean	Chicago, 14 February 1888
The Field	R. I. Pocock, 'A Lion Tiger Hybrid', 28 February 1929
The Gentleman's Magazine	July, 1793
The Journal of the Royal Asiatic Society	A. Buchthal, 'Indian Fables in Islamic Art', October 1941
Man	L. A. Cammiade, 'Man-Eaters and Were-Tigers', October 1931
Man in India	Asutosh Bhattacharyya, 'The Tiger Cult and its Literature in Lower Bengal', Vol. XXVII, 1947
Smithonian Magazine	Peter Jackson, 'Smithsonian Tiger Saving Operation', August 1979